KU-615-874

SURVIVING

Why We Stay and How We Leave Abusive Relationships

Beverly Gooden

sheldon^PRESS

Stockport Libraries

C2000003264068

First published in the United States in 2022 by Rowman & Littlefield,
an imprint of The Rowman & Littlefield Publishing Group, Inc.

First published in Great Britain by Sheldon Press in 2022
An imprint of John Murray Press
A division of Hodder & Stoughton Ltd,
An Hachette UK company

1

Copyright © Beverly T. Gooden 2022

The right of Beverly T. Gooden to be identified as the Author of the Work has been
asserted by her in accordance with the Copyright, Designs and Patents Act 1988.

All rights reserved. No part of this publication may be reproduced,
stored in a retrieval system, or transmitted, in any form or by any means
without the prior written permission of the publisher, nor be otherwise circulated
in any form of binding or cover other than that in which it is published and
without a similar condition being imposed on the subsequent purchaser.

This is a true story but in order to preserve the anonymity of some of the participants
involved, their names and identifying features have been changed.

A CIP catalogue record for this title is available from the British Library

Trade Paperback ISBN 978 1 529 39505 1
eBook ISBN 978 1 529 39507 5

Printed and bound in Great Britain by Clays Ltd, Elcograf S.p.A.

John Murray Press policy is to use papers that are natural, renewable and
recyclable products and made from wood grown in sustainable forests.
The logging and manufacturing processes are expected to conform
to the environmental regulations of the country of origin.

John Murray Press
Carmelite House
50 Victoria Embankment
London EC4Y 0DZ

www.sheldonpress.co.uk

For Nadia Ezaldein

ABOUT THE AUTHOR

Beverly Gooden is a writer, creative, and social activist known for her groundbreaking hashtag movement #WhyIStayed. *Surviving: Why We Stay and How We Leave Abusive Relationships* is her debut memoir. She earned a master's degree in social justice from Loyola University Chicago, where she wrote her thesis on institutional responses to single women experiencing intimate partner violence. Her writing has appeared in the *New York Times*, the U.S. Office on Women's Health, and *Time* magazine. She is a native of Cleveland, Ohio.

Beverly is the recipient of Investigation Discovery and *Glamour* magazine's Inspire A Difference "Everyday Hero" Award and was featured in a Toyota commercial discussing her work with survivors of intimate partner violence. In 2014, Beverly founded the Ella Mae Foundation, a philanthropic organization focused on intimate partner survivor health and wellness. Beverly also holds a bachelor's degree in journalism from Hampton University. She lives in Houston, Texas.

Visit her at www.beverlygooden.com.

CONTENTS

INTRODUCTION

In many ways, I still grieve my marriage, an entire decade after ending it. I still think about the what-ifs. What if I'd gone to therapy with him just a few more times? What if we'd chosen to have a prolonged separation period, followed by a restorative process that culminated in us renewing our vows? What if I'm wrong about how bad it was, now that I've seen more severe cases of physical abuse happen to others?

What if I had just stayed?

I have traveled around the country talking to people about the complexities of domestic violence. How sometimes there are red flags; sometimes there are none. How a person who is abusive carefully peels away the layers of confidence you have in your ability to make decisions, causing you to question reality. Is this real? Are they right? Are my feelings irrational? Am I being dramatic? How victims are so often dismissed by the public, accused of trying to ruin a person's life, or confronted with questions like "How do we know you're telling the truth?"

But I realized that even as I write these words in December 2020, exactly ten years removed from the marriage I left, I am gripped by how confusing it is to survive abuse. How every day in the relationship is a game of wits; who will outsmart who in the race to win control. I look in the mirror at my skin, knowing that as a Black woman, the severity of my experience will always be questioned, if taken seriously at all. And if I am believed, my strength might be hailed as valuable and I may even be called heroic, all while my vulnerability and pain goes overlooked.

So, the words that follow in this book will be deliberately vulnerable. I don't want you to see me as strong, even though that is true and something I value. I want you to see me as sensitive and delicate, capable of being harmed, in need of care and attention. I want you to see me as someone who survived, not because of any superhuman abilities, but because of intentionality, timing, will, and good luck. And I want these things because I want you to see survivors this way—as people who have, over time, had their agency removed by someone they love, and who have had to make difficult choices, some you agree with and many you might not, in an effort to reclaim power and reinvent themselves in order to live a full life.

This is not a traditional, triumphant love story as there is no new love at the end of this book. There is only me; *I am my triumphant love story*. So then, this book, what you will read, is my journey from choosing outwardly to choosing inwardly. Licking my finger, raising it in the air like a weathervane, determining the path of my own emotional winds and moving in the direction of *peace*. And I hope my journey propels you into a deep, abiding love for yourself. A love that exists even when life is bitter. A love that brings sweetness. A love that invites freedom. And a love that you, in all your power and autonomy, choose for yourself.

I hope that you are your happy ending.

Beverly Gooden

Part I

Chapter I

STUCK

"Our first responsibility in the midst of violence is to prevent it from destroying us."
—Henri Nouwen

The thing about abuse is that it creeps up on you. It's not a horror film where the villain sneaks up behind you in the night. It's more like a psychological thriller where the quiet, ever-present stock character is ultimately revealed as the orchestrator of chaos. You didn't see them coming.

It can be gradual, in the way that learning is. You start out with a bit of knowledge and, over time, discover more. You notice a few odd behaviors and, over time, they multiply. But by the time they multiply, it's too late.

You meet someone, and they take your breath away. Love is beautiful, life is looking super up. You have someone who *sees* you and wants to make you happy. And you want to be happy. You've been through some things in dating, and you're ready for whatever the New Moon brings you in love. And it has brought you this person—loving, beautiful, and very, very into you.

So into you that they want to be around all of the time. So into you that they always seem to pop up when you're spending time alone or with loved ones. Speaking of loved ones, they don't want you spending *too* much time with them because you should be focused on what the two of you are building. So into you that they really want to see your phone . . . and have your password. You know, just in case. So into you that they've begun to tell you who is bad for you, as in, who is out to "get you" (whatever that means). And it just so happens that everyone who is bad for you are the people that you love.

So into you that, in order to protect you from the bad people in your life, they start answering your phone and replying to your DMs. So into you that they accidentally pushed you during an argument. Accidentally, of course. Because they said it was an accident, and it's never happened before, so it was definitely an accident. So into you that . . . it happens again. Only this time the push is followed up with targeted insults about your hairstyle and the way you dress.

But they are sorry, so sorry, and so certain that it will never happen again, again. So sorry that they got you that Thing You Mentioned a few weeks ago because, look, they love you so much that they remember everything you say. You'd forgotten about that Thing You Mentioned, but they didn't, because they love you and are so sorry. Then a few months go by, and they were right, it hasn't happened again! And you're in love now. And it's beautiful now. So beautiful that they want to move in together. You think it's too soon, but why not? Life is about taking chances.

But not long after you're all moved in, they start going through your things. Reading your journals, looking at your phone when you're not in the room. And when you confront them about it, they say you're being too emotional, acting crazy or "always so sensitive." That they're not really going through your phone, they're watching YouTube videos on it because their phone is dead. You're wrong and being dramatic about it, despite you seeing them in your text messaging app with your own eyes. It feels wrong, but you don't know exactly how to identify what's wrong about it. Everything you've heard about abuse is that it's physical, and you don't have bruises, so it couldn't be abuse.

Then it happens again. That behavior they promised would never happen again, and hasn't happened again, happens again. But you're stuck this time. There is no going home this time because you are home. And your home is their home. You can't call a friend because if you do, they'll be even more mad. Plus, they have your phone. But after they calm down, another Thing You Mentioned appears and another "so sorry," and another "it won't happen again." But what won't happen again this time? The pushing or the spying? You don't even know anymore and, anyway, you just want some peace in your home. You forgive them and hope that things change for the better.

Or maybe none of that happens. Maybe you just know something is wrong; you can feel it. It could be that your partner sought a power imbalance early in the relationship and has held on to that control ever since, without apology. Maybe any level of manipulation or coercion is rarely present, but when it is you reel from it. Abuse is not a cycle, though it's been described that way in the past. Because if abuse were a cycle, it would be predictive. Those of us who have lived through it know that it can be anything but.

There can be recognizable patterns, but to say we can always identify those patterns, or that they follow a clear trajectory, is misleading. Abuse is an intentional action in an effort to wield control. Whether it happens once or is continual.

And any of it—physical, emotional, verbal, sexual, financial—is abuse.

The first thing I remember about that Saturday morning was falling. I felt unstable, as if I were on a rollercoaster ride making its first big dip, before I landed hard on my side. The beige Berber carpet softened my fall, so I wasn't hurt. But something still felt wrong.

I knew I hadn't just slipped off the bed. My husband, H., had pushed me.

But why? By now I'd have expected him to lunge across the mattress, shouting accusations, threats, or insults. Like the time he accused me of cheating on him with a friend of mine, or when he got mad because my V-neck top was too low cut and he said that I was trying to get attention from other men. Some reason, any reason to call me stupid or ridiculous. By now, I'd have known if I left a dish in the sink overnight, offending his ultra-orderly sensibilities, or if he was mad at someone else altogether and taking that anger out on me. By now, I'd have my answer.

Instead, there was nothing but silence. All I could hear was his slow and steady breathing on the other side of the room. I couldn't see him, but I knew he was there. Years of watching and anticipating his every move had taught me there was more to come.

My mind raced through the options. A hallway separated our bedroom and bathroom, and my side of the bed had a clear path to its entrance. It was the only room in the house that had a working lock, making it the best place to ride the storm of his temper out. But the floor next to where I'd landed had a creak in it, so he would know exactly when I was making my move. I had to be quick.

Carefully and quietly, I swung my legs around and pulled myself up into a kneeling position, placing my hands on the floor in front of me like a sprinter. Then, I started to run.

As I ran, I felt the whoosh of the cordless phone just missing my head before it hit the bedroom wall. Scared but not distracted, I made it to the bathroom, but not fast enough for me to close and lock the door. He pushed it open and, for the first time that morning, I saw the anger in his eyes.

My only defense was a pair of black, rainbow-patterned flip flops I kept by the tub. I grabbed one and threw it at him. As I bent down and reached for the second, he snatched my arm with one hand, gripped my neck with the other, and swung me against the bathroom wall. For a moment he pinned me there, leaving one of my arms loose.

Seizing the chance, I reached up to slap H. in the face, but my hand didn't connect. I did not normally return his violence with my own, so the fact that I was attempting to fight back only served to fuel his anger—and that's when he threw the first punch. Then I felt his grip tighten around my neck as he started to squeeze.

I closed my eyes and tried to focus on remaining conscious. My legs and arms weakened and my fingers, which had been wrapped around his forearm, went limp. One by one, my senses started to fade.

Then, just as quickly as it began, it ended without a single word. He released my neck and walked slowly out of the bathroom, his complete silence before, during, and after the violence just making that moment even more terrifying.

I collapsed onto the cold tile floor and took in deep, painful breaths. My lungs hurt from the massive effort to catch all that lost oxygen. Once I felt stronger, I reached over to the bathroom door, pushed it closed, and locked it, just in case. Sitting in silence, I listened for his next movements: a shuffling as he got dressed, that creak underneath the carpet as he walked out of the bedroom, the dark green apartment door slamming shut. Seconds later, the car engine roared into ignition, tires squealing as he sped away from our building.

I leaned my head back against the cream-colored vanity and surveyed the evidence of what had just happened: our toothbrush holder knocked off the sink, a twisted bath mat, our yellow hand towel surprisingly still hanging on its rack. I could taste the broken skin inside my mouth where he'd hit me, that sweet, warm slice of pain that is felt when you accidentally bite the inside of your cheek.

I felt a surge of emotion flow through my body, until finally, I started to cry.

Looking back on the beginning of our relationship, my biggest regret is not being able to stop the train at the first hint of danger.

My parents have been married for nearly forty-five years; that's a lot of pressure. Since college, relationships have been an odd needle for me to thread—the idea of dedicating my entire life to one person is frightening at best. I'm not a commitment-phobe, but I'm also not commitment prone. Love is something I've entered into infrequently and with great hesitation.

But when I'm in, I'm in.

You know how you know of someone, meaning they are always around in one way or another, but you've never interacted with them? That's how it was with H. We were in college in Virginia, me at Hampton University, a Historically Black College (HBCU), and he at a different local college that I visited often. He was always around, moving quietly through the motions of college—class, break, fast food for lunch, class, extracurricular activities, class, church, off-campus apartment, repeat. He was sort of closed off, socially. He had a few close friends that he opened up around, having out-of-earshot conversations with his big, beautiful smile and a warm laugh to match. But when they weren't around, he mostly stayed to himself.

The very first time I saw H., which I remember clearly, was at an evening church service where he performed with his musical group. He was directing the group from the piano, singing what he announced was an original song—a bright, energetic, up-tempo praise song with just two lines that repeat as the song modulates. It was good. I still remember it.

Unfortunately, I was attending that service with a guy I was dating, or so I thought. Turns out he'd been dating a few of us at school, but that's neither here nor there. What is here and there is that I couldn't speak with my future husband because my sometimes boyfriend was in the way.

Enter early social media.

A few weeks later, he posted the original song they'd performed at the church service on his MySpace page. I immediately commented on it—because it really was a great song and because I wanted to capture his attention. I said I loved the song; he replied, "Thank you Bev!"; and the rest is history.

Seriously, we were friends from that moment on.

Friends though, because finding a boyfriend wasn't my priority once I made it through freshman year. I dabbled in relationships when I wasn't busy unsuccessfully attempting to hold on to my academic scholarship. Otherwise, I was either on the music social scene or involved in the local community, volunteering to clean parks or plant trees with community groups or attending activist meetings off campus. A passion for social justice ran in my family.

So, we were cool—not dating, not sleeping together—when I decided to leave the area for grad school. In 2007, I moved to Chicago to start a graduate program in social justice at Loyola University in Chicago. My declared intention was to study issues of homelessness and housing. I really felt as if I'd found my purpose.

Living in Chicago was everything; I loved it from the start. Chicago is the perfect mix of professional, social, and cultural, and from the second I arrived there I thrived. I lived on campus in an apartment with other Loyola students, which was an adjustment since I'd been living on my own for two years after graduating from college. But I adjusted quickly, becoming close with my apartment-mates, making new friends in the grad school program, and reconnecting with childhood friends who also lived in Chicago. I dated a bit, but nothing serious.

It was during this time that my friendship with H. gradually took a romantic turn. He was still living in Virginia while I was in Chicago, but we texted every day and flirted on MySpace. I spent a lot of time writing papers, and he spent a lot of time writing music, but we never lost touch. He always made time for me.

Quiet and thoughtful, he openly admired my focus and seemed proud of my achievements. I was different from other women, he kept telling me.

"How?" I'd ask.

"I can't explain it. You're just special, you know?"

I didn't know, but now I do.

Everyone is special in their own way, but what I've learned now is that it's important to get clarification on what "different" means. Am I different in that I change my hairstyle twice a month—sometimes in a blonde wavy bob and other times, long black braids? Or am I different because I seem *super* forgiving, thus more likely to repeatedly forgive . . . you? People say things like "you're just different" without detailing what is different about us, what makes us special *to them*. I want to know exactly what is special or different about me to you so that I can understand the intent behind those words. But then, I was just giddy to be called "special" by someone I liked.

We had a magnetic draw to each other, even long distance. He was so introverted and reserved that it made me feel special that he made time to talk regularly. And then every day. And then multiple times a day! Then came the "good morning" texts, late night, three-hour phone calls where we'd barely stay awake, and finally the calls that didn't end, where we slept on the phone all night. Together.

It felt like one of those undeniable romances from films like *Brown Sugar* or *Sylvie's Love*. Both gradually and all at once, he had my heart. He *was* my heart. The kindest guy, plucked from the lines of the sweetest song just for me to sing. I was corny about H. I felt tingly sensations when I looked at a picture of him. Fluttery and unanchored, I got high on the goodness of being loved by him. And he was good at it, at loving me.

My dad has loved me in very specific ways. He shows his love by telling me "I love you," but also by anticipating my needs and taking action to ensure a positive outcome for me. H. showed love for me in precisely the same way. If I were writing a paper, he'd call to say he was not going to bother me for a few hours so I could get it done. Once I mentioned that my favorite pens were low on ink, and a week later, a new set of those pens arrived at my place. He knew I liked to work with background noise, so he made a playlist of ambient sounds—gentle rain, deep humming, and wind noise—for concentration. Loving me seemed like a task that came naturally to him.

We decided to meet up for a weekend in Virginia after a few months of very clearly falling for each other. I was nervous but certain—I knew his feelings for me were real. From the second I got off the plane to the moment I got back on, I had nothing but joy. He gave me a big, swinging hug when he picked me up from the airport, following by a long kiss. We had a great weekend. The day that I left for Chicago, we woke up early in the morning and sat on the beach together, taking photos and making promises.

"I'm going to marry you," he said. "You know that, right?"

"Yes," I said. I did know that. And I wanted that.

He did everything right, from posting love notes on my Facebook page to calling every night when he got home from work. We didn't see each other a lot because of the distance, but I always knew he would be there for me when I needed him. Caring and sweet, no one had ever made me feel more appreciated.

Looking back, I guess I was always drawn to H., even when the relationship was platonic. He was so fine—tall and muscular with intense brown eyes, a sharp jawline adorned with a neatly trimmed beard, and perfect skin, he looked as if he'd been gently formed with care by two potters who loved him deeply. But it was more than physical—it was his essence. His presence was charismatic, magnetic even. Every time he drew me into his chest for a hug, I melted, breathing him in. I loved the way his smile would light up his face when we saw each other on video chat at the end of a long day. This beautiful man loved me, and he was all mine.

So, when he asked me to move back to Virginia after months of long-distance dating, I didn't hesitate. I'd only been in Chicago a year, but I gave up my internship at the Alliance to End Homelessness, left my friends behind, and moved my few belongings across the entire country and into his little apartment.

It was 2008 and I'd been living with H. for two months when he told me to get dressed up and meet him at a fancy restaurant after work. He had already left by the time I got home from work—I'd landed a job at a nonprofit that coordinated grants for shelters—so I showered, put on a full face of makeup, and grabbed the nicest dress I had in our closet. We didn't have much living on a nonprofit salary and musician's gig pay.

When I walked into the restaurant, the host smiled big and asked me if my name was Beverly. When I said yes, she asked me to follow her and led me to where he sat, looking good but nervous. I saw that he'd already ordered a few appetizers, and I sat across from him.

"How was your day, boo?" he asked.

"It was good, but long," I answered. Just then the server walked gingerly up to our table, as if to not interrupt our conversation.

"Hi, Beverly!" she said, as I wondered why all of the people I'd interacted with so far knew my name. "We have some champagne on the way, but would you also like some water?"

"Yes, please," I said, suddenly worried about how we would pay for the champagne. Did H. order champagne? Did the restaurant just decide to give us some on the house? I decided I'd ask him once the server left our table, not wanting to talk money in front of her. As she began pouring the water, I noticed H. anxiously gesture toward the piano player in the middle of the dining room, rapidly twirling his hand as if to say, "Now!"

"What are you doing?" I asked, giggling at H. as the server lifted the water carafe and rushed away without saying anything.

And that's when I heard it.

Despite not being the healthiest film, the main theme song from *The Notebook* is, ironically, one of my favorite compositions. It begins slowly, in 4/4 time, a quiet piano solo in the high octaves of C Major, measured and sweet. It feels like a morning song; something birds would sing at dawn. A gentle "welcome to the day" from nature.

The piano player began to play the theme from *The Notebook* quietly, and I looked up at H. and said, "That's my favorite song!" H. smiled and took a long sip of his water. Without saying anything, he rose from his seat, took two steps over to my side of the dinner table, and got down on one knee. I froze, as I never know how to react to surprises well, but my heart began to beat rapidly, and my face grew hot—a mix of awkwardness from being the center of attention and excitement because he was very clearly proposing to me.

Everyone in the small restaurant turned to look at him, and I noticed he was sweating.

I stayed seated in my chair but turned toward him still kneeling on the restaurant's tile floor.

"Bevey, I love you. Will you spend forever with me?"

Have you ever wanted to cry—like, you knew the moment was made for crying but you were so distracted by your own thoughts that you couldn't focus on producing tears? This was that moment for me. What felt like a dozen emotions filled me up; I had nerves from the reality of being proposed to, something I'd always dreamed of. But I also felt suffocated by the public display itself; everyone was looking at me, waiting for my answer, and I hate public surprises. My entire body was shaking as he held my right hand; I looked at him while he waited for me to say something. But I felt excitement over the beautiful ring he held out in front of me.

Realizing I had just seconds to answer until things got awkward and knowing that I would definitely like to marry him, I quieted my thoughts and finally forced my lips to part open in order to say, "Yes."

I still remember how I felt when he slid the two-carat diamond ring on my finger. I loved him more than life; he was my heart and soul. Spend forever with you? Without question. Forsaking all others, for better or worse, in sickness and in health, 'til death do us part? Yes, please, all of that. Describing him as the "the man of my dreams" would have been an understatement. I couldn't even dream of a man so perfect.

Until he wasn't.

Maybe I should have known the relationship was wrong for me even before I accepted his proposal. Not long after I'd moved back to Virginia to be with H., before he proposed, he was violent for the first time. And the reason was so random and bizarre that I couldn't even wrap my head around it.

The first time he hit me was on my twenty-sixth birthday.

He'd decided to throw me a surprise birthday party, and as long as he'd known me, he'd never realized that I hate public surprises. Private ones are nice but public, *group* surprises? They're just not my thing. First of all, what if you don't like the surprise? You can't just say "ew" and leave. Second, say it's a proposal, and unlike me, the proposee doesn't want to marry you? Then you have to deal with the fallout of being rejected in public when you could've been rejected in private. And you already know the uncomfortable moment is somewhere on social media, immediately posted by a passerby for internet clout. You better hope it doesn't go viral.

But H. put his all into making the birthday party special for me, inviting a few of our mutual friends and his closest friends, choosing every detail from the balloons to a menu of the finest tacos in the Tidewater area, so I reacted with feigned excitement. In retrospect, I should have told him then that I hate public surprises, since my public proposal would soon follow.

H. had booked a beautiful hotel suite overlooking the beach in Virginia Beach and catered the party with some of my favorite foods—baked chicken, macaroni and cheese, key lime pie. It was so thoughtful and specific. It was an incredibly sweet gesture; he'd gone to the trouble because he wanted to make me feel welcome. I'd given up so much to move to Virginia to be with H. that it was his way of introducing me to his life and making me feel that his friends were my friends, too. I smiled, thanked, and hugged him, and greeted everyone who'd turned up for the celebration.

One of his closest friends at the party was a sweet guy with dusty brown hair and blue eyes named Derek. They had met in their music theory class back in college. According to H., Derek used to ask about me at the beginning of every class.

"He probably thinks you're fine," he said one day, after I asked how Derek was doing.

But at the party, I just thought Derek was being nice. I thought nothing of it. Nor did I think anything of the fact that Derek had brought me a birthday gift—a green handmade scarf.

"My mom makes these and sells them on eBay," he said. "He told me this is your favorite color."

I decided to wear Derek's scarf during the party to show my appreciation. I remember feeling happy and sociable that night. Most of my friends lived in Chicago, so it was my chance to get to know my boyfriend's friends a little better. We spent the evening drinking, laughing about his old professors, and I watched them randomly write songs, as music majors tend to do.

After everyone left, H. plopped down on the couch, grabbed the last bottle of wine, and took it to the head. I was still sober, but this didn't alarm me—we both loved cheap wine. And he'd just executed an amazing birthday party, which I was sure took a lot of work.

But there was something about his demeanor that seemed off. He had a deadened stare; his face was tight and drawn, as if the guy I knew and loved had disappeared behind a stony mask.

"You okay?" I asked him. He didn't respond. "Babe, are you good?"

"You embarrassed me."

"What? How?"

"You didn't show any appreciation for everything I did tonight."

I was grateful, and I said so. But I guess it wasn't the tears-of-joy reaction he'd been hoping for, and he was mad. It escalated from there.

"Why do you flirt with everyone all the time?" he asked.

My mind raced to figure out who I'd flirted with that evening. His friends? My friends? I had no clue.

"What are you even talking about right now? I wasn't flirting with anyone."

"Yes, you were. You always do. You love doing that."

Before I knew it, we were yelling at each other, his face just a couple of inches from mine. This went on for a few minutes, until I started to walk away.

In one quick movement, he reached for my throat, and I felt his fingers tighten around my neck. My petite 5'4" frame was powerless against his 6'3", 180-pound body. The scarf I had worn the entire night fell to the floor as he pushed me hard against the wall and started to choke me.

I froze. I had never been hit before. A jumble of thoughts raced through my mind. *He's going to let me go. He's not letting me go. I'm going to die tonight. My dad is gonna cry. Why hasn't he let me go yet? I love him.*

As soon as I was still, he let go of my throat and walked out the door. He was gone for about an hour, but I didn't run away. It was the shock of what just happened more than the physical pain that left me shaken, dazed, and sad. Physical violence had never happened at

home, in my family, or among my friends—at least, not that I knew
of. I knew this was bad, but I wanted to know why he'd do something like that.

When he came back, he was tearful, pleading for forgiveness.

"Baby, I am so, so sorry. I can't believe I did that. I swear to you
it will never happen again."

I didn't say anything. I just sat there looking at H., letting him
kiss my hands and lay his head on my lap. But it was exactly what I
needed to hear. During all the time I had known him, there was
never the slightest hint of a violent streak in this calm, pensive man.
He was a music nerd—gentle, soulful, and kind. No one who knew
H. would have believed this was possible. It had to be a mental lapse
fueled by too much wine and the pressure of all that party planning.
For a few minutes, a demon had possessed him, and now it was
gone.

Deep in my denial, despite the obvious red flags, I accepted his
apology. And a few months later, we were planning the wedding of
my dreams.

Of course, he did do it again. And again. And again. But the
violent moments were fast-moving episodes in between long
stretches of harmony. He showed me just enough affection between
the fights to keep me in a state of blissful self-delusion. He loved me
and would never intentionally do anything to hurt me seriously, I'd
convinced myself, rationalizing all the way. The math was still very
much in his favor.

And it's hard to know when it's time to give up, especially after
you've taken vows in front of God and two hundred hungry wedding guests. Once we were married, there was no turning back. I
was the ultimate "for better or worse" woman. I grew up in the
church, and there was no way I could get divorced with a straight
face. Marriage was a holy union. My parents were one of my marital
role models, and I was determined to follow in their footsteps. I
believed I could fix this, that by acting a certain way, I could convince H. to change.

I stopped wearing low-cut tops, donating most of the ones I
already owned, and started wearing crew-neck tops and turtlenecks.

I became a tidiness addict, making sure everything in our home was in the exact place he liked, or in the place I'd designated for it. I cleaned our home *incessantly* because he was the most sanitary person I'd ever met. I'm talking bleaching the bathtub several times a week whether one of us used it or not, and constantly disinfecting every item in our kitchen. I stopped talking to anyone H. didn't like, including friends I'd had for years.

We were both seeking control of the relationship. My husband used fear; I used my ability to read the signs and modify my behavior accordingly. In a sick way, I took some satisfaction in knowing that I had the power to manage my husband's emotions. It was kind of a thrill. I've got this, I told myself.

Until I realized that wasn't true. Until I realized that I couldn't time or predict his violence. I couldn't provoke it or defend myself against it.

I was not in control.

I was so traumatized that I began to disassociate. I detached myself from the physical and emotional pain so much that the incidents became a blur. It was easier to get through the day by compartmentalizing—I still find myself compartmentalizing, even now. When something is too stressful or causing too much internal commotion, I imagine myself picking it up, moving it aside, and continuing on. It's almost creepy the way I've adapted to pushing through stressful situations with no measure of self-care. It's a tactic that so many survivors developed—in order to make it through the day, you keep your head down and make magic happen. Back then I would tell myself, "No, that didn't just happen," or, "He didn't mean it; it won't happen again," to push through the day. Facing the truth that the person I loved most wanted to hurt me sometimes was simply too much to accept.

I blocked it all out.

I also had the sense that I'd invested so much time, energy, and emotion into the relationship that throwing it all away felt like a huge loss. Economists call this the sunk-costs fallacy; it originally referred to business investments in which the cost has already been incurred and can't be recovered, like a ship that sank with all its treasures and is now sitting at the bottom of the sea. An entrepreneur might say, "I've already put $100,000 into this new app, but nobody is downloading it. I don't want to write it off, so I'll keep pushing this app until I start to see a return on my investment." Nobody wants to download that app, and the rational choice is to walk away, but the entrepreneur can't accept that it's a lost cause and keeps throwing good money into a bad product.

The sunk-costs fallacy can apply to any relationship that's wrong for us, both abusive and nonabusive. In my life, it was abusive. But in the lives of others, it can just be a relationship that's not working. *Washington Post* business reporter Megan McArdle discovered this when she broke up with her boyfriend. He was a nice guy and he treated her well enough, but for three years he just would not commit. The signs were always there, but she ignored them, believing she could persuade him into monogamy. When she was finally confronted head-on with the truth—that he just didn't love her the way she loved him—she ended it. She spent months mourning the loss of the relationship until she realized she was doing the very thing she wrote about on her economics beat.

"I just couldn't let go and say, you know what? I invested all this time, and he's great, but this relationship is not going anywhere, and I have to let it go and go look for one that is," McArdle explains.[1]

Another thing that kept me stuck was guilt and shame, two things I'll get deeper into later in this book. But I felt so stupid, as if I'd gotten caught in a sucker's game when I should have known better. I never told a soul what was going on at the time because I was embarrassed. Most of my friends were coupling up and making progress in their lives. My God-fearing parents had been happily married for close to forty years at that time, and I couldn't bear the thought of disappointing them.

Some of that sense of failure stemmed from my belief that I should have been able to manage and fix things on my own. Had I done or said something differently, I could have avoided the blows; I was the trigger, the cause of all his anger. That was what he told me, and that was what I told myself. I wanted to believe it, because that meant it was in my power to make things better. The truth was,

I had no power in the relationship. Nothing I could have said or done differently would have changed his behavior. He simply would have adapted and attributed blame for the abusive behaviors to something *else* I did. I was not in control of things.

I wanted to feel the tenderness I'd felt when we first fell in love. I craved those moments, which often came by design; H. would give them to me whenever he could feel me slipping away. Once, after hitting me in the back of the head, I came home to find a trail of rose petals leading to the bed, where a heart formed out of rose petals was in the center. A gifted musician, he wrote love songs for me all the time. He was the perfect amount of affectionate yet firm, like a skilled massage therapist building up a satisfying experience of pressure and ease. I could always count on H. to hold my hands in his, kiss them, and tell me how much he loved me, for no reason at all.

Even when I started to see how scarce those moments had be-come—even when I finally gained the mental clarity to realize I was stuck in his game—I realized I was in so deep that life had effective-ly become a jail. I was completely isolated. We had moved far away from my family and friends, so finding a couch to sleep on wasn't just a matter of driving to the other side of town. Everyone in our social circle were his friends, not mine. All our nearby family members and fellow church congregants in Virginia belonged to H. as well. Eventually, he didn't want me to work, so I had no job, no separate source of income, and all of our finances were joint. I didn't have a lick of furniture or a cent to my individual name.

Toward the end, these were my main barriers against leaving. But throughout most of my marriage, the number one reason for staying was much more powerful: love.

Although practical considerations like finances play a role in staying in abusive relationships, we do the human heart an injustice by limiting the causes to economics alone. It's not easy to leave someone you love, fear, or both. It's not easy to leave when nostal-gia knocks on the door of your mind with instant replays of "the good old days"—when they treated you like a rare flower, touching you with care and making sure you were protected. H. and I frequently went to the beach to just chill, sitting on a blanket and dreaming up our future together, enjoying the ocean breeze. We'd always find something fun to do on Saturdays—riding rented bicycles or seeing a movie.

It's not easy when your partner promises it's the last time, because you believe in love, and you believe in them. Sometimes we forget that love is an incredibly powerful emotion. It overrides everything.

In an article for *Psychology Today*, Dr. Craig Malkin points to a photo essay by photographer Sara Naomi Lewkowicz, of a couple caught in an unhealthy relationship that showed the pair as they progress toward the next flare-up. The anger and aggression build up slowly, but in between, there is love—all those tiny moments of tenderness and vulnerability that we live for. "Those snapshots are poignant reminders of what abuse victims hold onto in staying with their abuser," says Malkin. [2]

My head was full of those tender images during the time when I was deciding to stay with H. Even now, I can recall in vivid detail how he wooed me; I still get goosebumps when I think about those early days. The flowers he sent along with handwritten cards. The random "I love you" voice messages. The original songs he wrote and named "Beverly 1" or "Beverly 2."

H. was the one person I talked to daily. My social interactions were superficial and restricted to folks like the cashier at the supermarket, his work colleagues, or various members of the church we attended. For days at a time, he was often the only voice I heard. We were in this together. The dysfunction in our marriage was our shared secret. We had developed this twisted codependency. I needed his near *constant* endorsement on everything, the clothes I'd wear and even the food I ate. And he needed to be needed by me. If I ever failed to ask for his opinion on something, that was considered a slight. I needed him to approve of me, and he needed me to revere him.

I looked forward to Sundays because I loved being part of a congregation. Whatever was going on in my home, communion with others helped me see the bigger picture—that this was not all there is. It gave me hope and a couple of hours of peace during the weekend, when he was home from work and monitoring my every move. And I liked the pastor, despite all his fire and brimstone, until one day he gave a sermon on divorce.

"Now y'all know God hates divorce!" he roared, in that big, preachery voice that pastors do. "Whatever is going on in your marriage, you don't get divorced. Divorce is a sin that violates God's law."

He backed it up with scripture, 1 Corinthians 7:10–11 NIV: "To the married I give this command (not I, but the Lord): A wife must not separate from her husband. But if she does, she must remain unmarried or else be reconciled to her husband. And a husband must not divorce his wife." Or Mark 10:12 NIV: "And if she divorces her husband and marries another, she commits adultery." Anyone can back anything with scripture when it's taken out of context, but this man was so convinced of its truth he had me questioning my relationship with God. How could God want this for me? How was I supposed to love and trust a God who hated what might be best for me?

Now I was really confused. Until then, it had never occurred to me that God might hate divorce more than physical abuse. The pastor's words rang through my head for the rest of the day, reinforcing this formerly devout church girl's fear of disappointing her Lord and Savior.

By then, my inner turmoil had reached a fever pitch. I'd been dancing with the idea of leaving but saw so many obstacles in my way—literally. One time after an argument, the origins of which I can't remember, H. slept across the threshold of our front door—the only way out of our apartment unless I was willing to jump from a third-story window.

I decided to put the idea of escape out of my mind. We'd both heard the divorce sermon, so maybe I could convince H. to go to couples therapy with me.

To my surprise, he agreed.

When we walked into the marriage counselor's office, I was full of hope. The counselor asked me to describe what was happening in our marriage, and I told him everything—the fighting, the hitting, the choking, everything. For the first time, I told someone outside our marriage about the violence; saying it out loud made it a blunt reality.

Then he chimed in with his take. "Yes, I hit her," he said. "But it's not abuse. We're just having some issues."

Sitting cross-legged on a leather sofa chair in front of us, his wood-paneled office lined with books, the marriage counselor started scribbling notes. After my husband finished explaining his side, the counselor breathed out a heavy sigh. Then he looked up at us, frowning.

"I think you two need to take a break," he began. "Hitting is not okay. And that lets me know you need time apart to figure things out."

I felt hopeful.

"But," he continued, turning to look at me. "While you're taking time apart, you need to figure out ways to get H. not to hit you."

I was stunned. Did he just tell me I had to figure out how to get my husband to stop putting his hands on me? Had he heard all the facts, an admission from my husband, and then told me to my face that it was my fault?

"Something you're doing is causing H. to react this way toward you," he continued. "I'm not sure what it is, but you've gotta figure that out. I can work with you both to figure that out, separately and as a union."

His reaction fed into all the justifications that my husband gave to absolve himself and make *me* think I'd done something to provoke the violence: wearing V-neck shirts, spending too much time on Facebook, inadvertently looking in the direction of a random man in the street. The absurdity of the counselor's words got my wheels turning, but in the opposite direction.

I began to realize there was *nothing* I could do to stop the abuse. H. would get mad and hit me even if I was completely silent, he'd always find a reason to be angry. Yet it was as if this counselor had permitted H. to continue hitting me. Over the next thirty minutes, the resounding theme of our counseling session was that I was at fault, and therefore in control. That I could control whether he hit me.

But that is not the nature of abuse. Abuse is not an action/reaction dynamic. Abuse is a choice that an abuser makes.

I thought about leaving many times but only acted twice.

He was a jealous guy, almost from the beginning. A few months after we started dating, when I was still living in Chicago, a childhood friend of mine named Alex was in town for a music gig. It was our custom that whenever one of us was in the other's city, we'd support whatever the visit was for and then hang out all night. This only happened once a year or so, and it was something I always looked forward to.

When I told H. that my friend would be in town, he got mad. "Does he like you?" he asked.

The truth is, there had been a time years before I met H. that I had feelings for Alex. But it wasn't something I discussed with Alex, and I damn sure wasn't going to talk about that with my boyfriend. To complicate things, I thought—but wasn't sure—that Alex might also have had feelings for me at one point. Since the situation was clearly ambiguous, as many college-age situations are, I simply said, "No, I don't think so."

I only mention that moment as a precursor for what would happen a year later.

Over time, H. granted himself decision-making power over who I spoke to, why, and when. I was allowed to speak to my parents and my brother, any time except late evening when my attention was to be 100 percent on him. I was allowed to speak to what few friends I had left, all women, during the day only. I was never allowed to speak to men or make new friends that he did not already know. And I followed these rules, not out of subservience, but to keep the peace. I should say that an error in thinking that I had until this relationship was that if my partner wasn't hitting me, then nothing was wrong. Now, I know that's not true. I didn't know that then. Or rather, I didn't *understand* that then.

Both of us had wanted a big wedding because we had close families and loved a party. My lack of deep friendships—because he had become my only friend—and his choice to spend most of his time in my business, as opposed to nurturing his friendships, complicated that Big Wedding goal. What I'm saying is, we didn't have many friends! Not many to invite and not many to ask to be in the wedding party. Both of us started digging deep into our DMs and text messages to see who we could connect with enough to ask to be in the wedding. I was better at this, probably because I tried my best to at least stay in touch with old friends, even if I couldn't connect on a deeper level because of his ever-present listening ear. After a few weeks of digging, I'd produced six bridesmaids.

To his two groomsmen.

"Terrence can be #3. Do you want me to ask some of my old friends?" I asked H. one day while we were eating dinner.

"What old friends?"

"You know, some college friends."

He looked up, confused.

"What college friends are you still talking to?"

Well, that was a mistake.

"I'm not talking to any college friends, but I can reach out to them if you wanna get more people to be groomsmen."

"Give me some names."

It was more of a challenge than a request.

"You know the names already. Cliff, Marquise, Roy . . ."

"Roy."

I looked down at my food.

"It's always about Roy, isn't it?"

Now, I did have a crush on Roy in the past. I probably, at this exact moment, *still* had a crush on Roy. But you are allowed to have crushes on people; it does not make you morally bankrupt.

Regardless of my probable crush, I wasn't talking to Roy, seeing Roy, having sex with Roy, or cheating with Roy. In fact, I hadn't even spoken to Roy in months because H. made me cut him off. But the friendship I had with Roy was real; he was one of my closest friends before I started dating H. My parents loved Roy. We shared so much deep stuff with each other, from school mess to church drama, and I considered him to be an important part of my life until H. entered the picture.

"No, it's not," I said while still looking down. "It's about our wedding and your side of the aisle not looking empty."

I could see his anger building, and I was not in the mood to argue, so I quickly said, "Anyway, what do you want to do about the photographer?"

Redirection worked in those tense moments, but the thing about H. was that he *never* forgot.

The evening and following morning went smoothly. We only had one car at that time, so he dropped me off at work and, with a kiss, left to get to his job on time. I got a text from him midmorning asking if he could take me to lunch.

"Of course, babe!" I texted back.

At noon, I headed downstairs to meet him for lunch, and he was there waiting in the car for me, smiling. Everything seemed perfectly normal. I got in the car with him, and that's when it started.

"I read your journal today."

I froze.

"What?"

"I read your journal. I took it from your nightstand drawer and read it today. And you know what I saw?"

I knew what he saw. I'd had that specific journal for years and in it, I'd written about several guys. One of those guys was Roy.

No one, not even my parents, read my journal. I've been writing since I was a kid, and it's a part of me that I'm hesitant to share, which is kind of ironic now, as I'm writing this book. But back then, at that moment, it was a violation of my privacy. It felt different than any other violation; the most delicate, vulnerable parts of me had been projected onto a wall, from the pages that held my secrets.

"You told me you didn't like Roy, that's what you told me," he said. "You told me you've never kissed Roy."

"I haven't kissed Roy," I stated firmly.

"But you wanted to. You said that you wanted to."

My head was spinning. I couldn't gather any meaningful thoughts. I felt suspended in that moment, looking at myself from outside of myself. It was more about the violation than the argument. I could not move past it.

"Why would you read my journal? Why would you do that?"

"Because I knew you were lying," he said. "You always lie about him."

"This is stupid," I said.

"You saying I'm stupid?" he yelled.

That's not what I said, but he heard what he wanted.

"No, I . . ." before I could finish my sentence, he reached across my chest and pulled the passenger door handle. The door flew open, and he shoved me to push me out of the car.

"Get out!" he screamed, as the car kept moving.

When some chilling moment happens, many people say things like "It happened so fast." This literally happened so fast. There were only seconds between an argument and being pushed out of a moving car, and I felt like I was just floating in that space, grounded only by the wind that gently traced my right side, reminding me that in that moment, I and it, were still here.

The only thing saving me was my seatbelt. As he kept pushing, I kept grabbing for my door, but in a bizarre, dream-like moment born only of the immediate trauma, I considered unbuckling my seatbelt and falling out of the car just to get away from him.

Suddenly, he pulled over and slammed the brakes. My door was still open. When I turned to get out, I saw a postal courier, a Black woman, standing in front of a blue mail receptacle and looking at the car. He was yelling something inaudible to me; I was still in that dream-like state but, this time, grounded by the penetrating eyes of the postal courier staring directly into mine.

"Do you need help?" she asked me. It was a quiet ask, as if she understood the severity of the moment.

I shook my head no, but she kept staring at me. "Are you sure?"

"She don't need any fucking help," he yelled at her, reaching across my chest again, this time slamming the car door shut. He put the car in drive and pulled away, as I held eye contact with the postal courier. I told her no because I didn't know where a "yes" would lead. I didn't want to be in a shelter or to talk to the police. I didn't want to not go home after work or face the questions I'd get at a hospital. I just wanted to get out of the car.

I still think about that postal worker though. I wish she knew that I made it out alive.

We both sat in complete silence while he drove me a few blocks back to my office. Once he stopped at the curb in front of my office, I flung my seatbelt off and jumped out of the car, nearly running toward my building's door. He didn't wait to make sure I got in; I could hear him pull away before I even got inside.

I was not crying, but my shirt was wrinkled and twisted from the seatbelt. I got into the empty elevator and tried to smooth out my top, mind racing for an explanation should any of my coworkers ask about it.

When the elevator stopped on my floor, my boss was standing at the door, entering as I exited. I smiled and said, "Have a good lunch!"

"You're back really soon," she replied. "You're not going to get any food?"

"No, I'm okay," I said.

"Alright, well, let me know if you want me to bring you anything."

I walked to my cubicle and sat down, finally able to catch my breath.

The next few days were filled with silence. But I loved the silence because it gave me an opportunity to feel things fully, without the distraction of his presence.

I decided to remove all my books and journals from our apartment and put them into a small storage unit. I never wanted to feel violated in that way again. In fact, I haven't kept a journal since that day.

While he was at work that Saturday, I packed everything into a plastic storage bin and moved it into a storage unit I'd rented earlier that year, when we were in the midst of a move but unsure where we'd end up living. Not long after I returned home, he called me.

"My sister wants me to stop by so I can see her new car," he said.

"Okay." I knew that meant that I had to go too, because he rarely left me alone at night.

I took a shower and got dressed in what he deemed appropriate family visit attire—loose jeans, a modest sweater, simple earrings. I was trained by this point; I knew exactly how he wanted me to look based on the occasion.

When we got to his sister's house, he put the car in park and asked if I was coming in.

"No, I'll stay here" I said.

"Why?"

"I just don't feel like getting out."

"Alright, I'll be right back."

I watched as he walked to his sister's door, waited, and went inside. A few minutes later they both emerged, smiling. He loved his sisters; they had a tight bond.

I never got to see the new car because I feel asleep in his car a few minutes after they came back out of the house. I woke at the sound of his driver's side car door closing.

"Why you so tired?" he asked.

"I don't know," I said.

"You don't know or you don't want to say?"

"Please don't start an argument tonight, you see I'm tired," I replied, annoyed.

"Why you got an attitude? I'm just trying to see what's wrong with you."

I said nothing and closed my eyes again.

"So you're ignoring me now?" he said, determined to start a fight.

"No!" I yelled this time.

The movement was so fast that I didn't even see it coming.

He grabbed the left side of my head in his hand and slammed it onto the passenger window.

I didn't move. I couldn't move. With the right side of my temple pressed firmly against the cold window, I focused on breathing.

In. Out. One more time. In. Out.

He'd let me go soon. He'd be sorry soon. He'd hug me soon.

He let go of my head and opened his door to get out.

"Stay in the car."

I didn't respond.

As soon as he was out of eyesight, I opened my door, closed it gently behind me, and began to walk.

I didn't know exactly where I was going. Didn't have a plan. Just away from him. I knew at some point we would have to face each other again, and that terrified me. But I wasn't worried about that now. I just wanted to be escorted into the unknown by the darkness.

I cut across the parking lot and headed toward the nearby main street. A cat walked in front of me, and normally my reaction would be to jump. But I didn't. Nothing scared me anymore, not really. No one thing could hurt me more than he had.

As I started walking down the main street, I kept looking behind me afraid that he'd catch up after he realized I'd left. Sure enough, I watched a dark Nissan hit a fast U-turn ahead of me. He pulled up in the car in front of me and I quickly about-faced to walk in the opposite direction.

"Baby, it's dangerous over here. What are you doing?" he asked.

I said nothing.

"Get in the car, Stinky. I'm sorry."

"No."

"Baby, I'm sorry, okay? Just please get in the car, you could get shot walking out here."

"Get in the car and do what?" My face was hot with tears at this point. "Fight again?"

"Fight no more," he said, with certainty. "This is it, that was the last time. I promise, baby. I'll never do that again, okay? Please get in the car."

I shook my head and kept walking, laughing at myself through the tears. Nothing was funny, it's just that he'd said similar things before. I knew what this was. I knew he'd do it again.

"I'm not leaving you here, so I can ride slowly by you all night if you want."

The street, a main street in Virginia Beach, was oddly quiet. One or two cars drove past during this whole conversation. I looked down the street and saw nothing but darkness. Beside me was H., riding slowly as I walked. What am I even doing? I had $3 in my purse, no clue where I was going, or where the nearest gas station was.

I knew I could not leave him that night.

I knew I was stuck.

Chapter 2

CHOICES

"i am mine. before i am ever anyone else's."
—Nayyirah Waheed

We moved to Texas in 2010, thousands of miles away from friends, family, and acquaintances. By then we were married, and H. got an offer for a decent job, so I gave up my nonprofit career to become a stay-at-home wife at his request. I was still working in the housing field, writing grants and coordinating the Point-In-Time count for the Virginia peninsula area. I figured it wouldn't be too hard to find another nonprofit job if I needed to, but the way he put it, he wanted to take care of me. Now I know that the relocation made me even more stuck. No job and not a soul who knew me—except for H. And now I was all his.

The bad times started to outnumber the good. He left for work early in the morning and intentionally took the only car we had; if I had no transportation, then I had no independence. He was in constant contact with me from the moment he arrived at work—wake-up calls, text messages, surprise lunchtime visits, more text messages, emails from his professional account. He wanted to know what I was doing every second of the day. If I took the dog for a walk, he wanted to know how long I'd been away from our apartment. If the dishes weren't clean when he got home, he wanted to know what I'd been doing in the hour or so we hadn't spoken. It was a soft captivity that gave the illusion of freedom but, in reality, just trapped me. I was torn between trying to fix things and walking away, although, I was not seriously considering walking away.

A person who abuses is not always abusing. Most of the time, at least in the beginning of our relationship, we were fine. We still enjoyed each other's presence, still had a lot of fun. We still went to see movies, sat by the lake, and cuddled, took long drives after he got home from work, laughing and listening to music. But the seasoning in the pot of abuse—the things that aren't necessarily considered violent but are harmful and, at times, abusive in other ways—was always in the mix. That means yelling and cursing, controlling behaviors such as monitoring my phone use and telling me what to wear, popping up at unexpected times not as a surprise, but as surveillance. Those things were present in between moments of physical violence. Since these interactions are nonphysical, we tend to underestimate the harm that nonphysical violence can cause.

Getting out of an abusive relationship is a process; you can't just flip a switch. It's even harder when you're living in fear, which is one reason why domestic violence myths—that a victim can easily walk away, that "real" abuse is only physical, that violence must not be that bad if a victim stays—are so prevalent: People don't know what it's like to live in this state. I was betrayed by the person I loved most and stripped of autonomy and dignity. As time went on, dysfunction became the new normal. I couldn't even tell what a healthy relationship looked like anymore. Abuse is confusing. From beginning to end, I could not understand why my husband would do something like that to me. And I wanted to understand; I was curious about it.

He and I had a lot in common. We both grew up in church and in musical families. My mother has been a choir director my entire life. His father was a preacher, and his family had their own church. And since we went to college in the same area, we knew a lot of the same people.

When we first hooked up, he'd just ended a five-year relationship with a woman who lived in his area of Virginia. I never thought to reach out to her after our relationship turned violent, because he told me she was "crazy." Sometimes I wonder what sort of things he's told others about me now that I've left. Has he called me crazy too?

I hadn't been dating anyone, as I mentioned before. In fact, I did not have many serious post-college relationships. My first love was a guy that I dated in high school who died suddenly of a heart attack while playing basketball. I don't think I had recovered from that completely, and that relationship was the source of many arguments we would have. He'd tell me that I still loved my high school boyfriend, even though he was gone and very clearly not a threat. When he was angry one time, he threw away all my photos of my high school boyfriend. I remember it clearly because of the emotional pain, knowing I'd never get copies of those photos again since they were taken in the pre-digital age. How can you be jealous of a dead person? That always confused me. Now I know it wasn't just jealousy; it was also control. He wanted to be the only person who evoked buttery feelings of love from me. He wanted my complete attention. Another man, dead or alive, was a distraction from the life we were creating together. While my high school love wasn't a threat to our relationship, he was a threat to H.'s dominance.

In the beginning, we rarely fought at all. Our first real fight was about jealousy. He hated when I spoke to or spoke of any other man. This even included my cousins, who I've always been close to. The only exception was my brother Terrence, who is also my closest friend. He never punished me for my close relationship with Terrence. Maybe he knew that would be my breaking point.

And I don't think he wanted me to break. He only wanted me to have enough broken parts for him to play fixer. To be my personal mechanic, constantly refurbishing my heart—replacing the parts he'd shattered with new parts that he'd designed, until there was nothing left of the original me.

But I was a fighter back then—not physically, but I would verbally spar with him, so our conflicts were never really resolved. We would argue for hours, and then one of us would walk away. When he started to hit me is when I began to withdraw. I would stop arguing and crawl into a figurative, emotional hole to keep from being hit. I would do anything not to be hit. If it meant saying I was wrong or begging for forgiveness, I would do it—it did not matter.

My favorite time of day was when he was sleeping. Sometimes I'd lay awake and watch him, because in that moment he was quiet. And nonviolent. I could think clearly when he was sleeping. I could be present with my emotions without worrying he'd ask, "What are you thinking about?" That question could lead to my thoughts being targeted for a fight. When he was sleep, I could be me.

I wanted to be me when he was awake, too.

Waiting for the right moment to leave an abuser is an incredibly transgressive act. When I think about the choice to stay, and subsequently the choice to leave, I think about how it was less about physically getting away and more about restoring faith in my own decision-making abilities. I was asking myself: What is best for me at this moment? What is real and what is not real? Is the danger real? Yes. Is the idea that I can't make it on my own without H. real? No. So I stay for now because of that fear of danger. But I plan to leave later because I have confidence in myself and power to reinvent my life, without this relationship.

A few people had the opportunity to help me leave the relationship but chose not to. Looking back on it, I still question why they didn't try to help me more.

One hot summer afternoon before we'd moved to Texas, we had been arguing, for what reason I don't remember. After a while the "reasons" mattered less. What I do remember is walking into the bedroom and getting in bed, while he trailed behind me drinking a glass of water, fussing about whatever. He said something; I snapped back with something. Then that glass of water he'd been holding splashed in my face.

I was angry. Not only was I wet from H. throwing water in my face, but the bed was wet and whatever thing he was mad about wasn't resolved. I got out of the bed and walked past him to the bathroom to get a towel. I heard him grab his keys and walk out of the door, which was his move when he was angry but not angry enough to do more damage.

After I dried off, I called his cousin. His cousin had always been sweet to me; she'd been helping plan our wedding and checked in on us every few weeks.

"Hey, Bev. How are you?"

"Not good," I answered, honestly. "Your cousin threw water in my face, and I think I need help."

She was quiet. "Is he there right now?"

"No, he left."

"Where did he go?"

"I have no idea. Can you come and get me?" It was more of a beg than a question. Please, come get me.

"I don't have my car right now, but I'll call my husband and ask him. I'll call you back in a few minutes."

"Okay."

"Just pray. This is the devil testing you guys because he doesn't want you to be married. You are a powerful couple, and this is just Satan trying to break you apart."

"Okay."

I hung up the phone, packed a suitcase, and waited. And waited.

A few hours later, H. walked through the door.

"Where are you going?" he asked, gesturing at my suitcase.

"Trey is coming to get me," I said.

"No, he's not. He called me and we spoke."

"What did he say?"

"We're gonna hang out tomorrow and talk some more." I couldn't figure out what this had to do with Trey coming to get me.

I called his cousin back and she didn't answer. I called again after a few minutes.

"Hey, Bev. Is he back?"

"Yeah, he's here. Is Trey on his way? I'm scared."

She hesitated. "He's not coming. He called and spoke with H.," she said. "He's really sorry and just got caught up in the moment. He won't do it again. They're gonna get together tomorrow for dinner and to have some prayer."

"No one is coming to help me?" I asked, hot tears started to replace the cold water I'd wiped away earlier.

"It'll be okay. Just pray."

I sat in the emergency room intake chair and listened as the nurse asked me a series of questions about my frequent migraines.

"Can you rate the pain on a scale of one to ten?"

"Eight."

"Can you describe the pain? Is it stinging, throbbing, constant?"

"Throbbing."

"Are you experiencing domestic violence?"

I paused. "No."

I was experiencing domestic violence, but I was not yet ready to admit it. I was not ready to leave. At best, a premature move could handicap me financially. At worst, it could cost me my life.

Staying was a tough choice, but it was the best option for me. Living in Texas, cut off from friends and family, with no job and not even a bank account of my own, how would I leave? What would it take to start over?

Leaving was a process, not an event. I needed a place to go, a way to get there, housing, employment, and time. I just needed time. Because it's more than just *feeling* ready. You have to *be* ready.

It's hard to know when it's time to give up on a relationship, right? Well, it's even harder when you're living in fear. As time goes on, the violence becomes your new normal. You don't even know what a healthy relationship looks like anymore.

But after the morning that he woke me up by pushing me out of the bed, something shifted inside me. I knew there was no turning back. Usually, I could think of something I'd done or said to spark his temper, but this time, I'd been sleeping. What could I have done to piss him off so strongly this time?

The fights that had always seemed predictable became unpredictable. In normal times I could calculate when a simple disagreement was going to turn into an argument, and when that argument would take a turn for the worst. The blank look in his eye, the way his eyebrows rose sharply and then slanted when his temper began to flare. How his voice fell into a deep speaking range if he was getting upset. Those few seconds of complete silence that typically preceded physical aggression. My husband's rapid escalation to violence that morning revealed a total lack of control over his anger. He'd hit me many times before and it hurt, but until that morning it had never crossed my mind that he might kill me. And the unpredictable moment made it seem like death might be a possibility one day.

I believe we all have moments when the truth is so clear that it becomes undeniable. It shakes us to our core. And it can hurt like hell because it means the loss of the life we've been clinging to. In a way, it's the death of your old self. However, it's also a rebirth. You've known you were stuck for a long time, but now you recognize that you don't have to be forever. And this is when you tell yourself: It ends now. I fight back now. I get away now. I breathe now. I create a new life. Now.

I woke up that morning, both literally and figuratively. This time, I knew beyond a shadow of self-doubt that I had a choice to make: Either stay in the marriage and risk dying by my husband's hands, or walk away and live.

That morning in the bathroom, I chose to live.

I'd been holding my breath for too long, burying myself for the sake of peace. I was ready to nurture a new life based on a sense of wholeness and security. The fact that I had no idea how I would leave, or what exactly it would take to start over again, wasn't going to stop me. I'd had my epiphany and I would never be the same again. I became *laser-focused* on my goal to reclaim my identity and to live life on my terms.

It was around this time that I finally called my parents and told them what my husband had been doing to me. The first thing my mother said was, "Oh no." That "oh no" was a complete, heavy sentence, a vocal mourning of the twenty-seven-year-old dream that their daughter would marry someone who treated her well, was gentle with her, and gave her everything he had.

Instead, the person with whom they'd entrusted their daughter's life abused not only their daughter, but their trust. Months later, my father would mention to me that he had "lost a son." In all that time, I'd never thought about how hard a situation like this could be on the people close to those living through abuse, but it became clear that my loss was their loss. And the emotional pain extended beyond just the two people in the relationship; it impacted those who loved them too.

On my wedding day, my dad and I had stood next to each other, his arm in mine, waiting in the church vestibule outside the sanctuary behind big, brown double doors. I'd been sweating since I put the white dress on—a dress that my fiancé had made me show him before I bought it. But I don't think it was the sweat that caught my dad's attention; my arm was shaking.

"Are you sure?" my dad asked, looking over.

"Yes, I'm sure, Daddy."

And I *was* sure—excited, nervous, happy, hopeful—though I was answering a question my father didn't exactly ask.

I was sure that my fiancé would change, as he'd promised. At this point, he'd been hitting me for more than a year.

Two days earlier, I had missed my early morning flight from Virginia Beach, where my fiancé and I shared an apartment, to my hometown of Cleveland where all my family lived for our wedding. I'd overslept and hadn't packed the night before my flight. Now that I think about it, my laziness in the days leading up to that flight was my intuition in overdrive, exhausting itself while fighting to convince me not to marry this man.

My fiancé had driven me to the airport, both of us praying that the flight would wait on me. It didn't—probably another sign from the universe—and I stood in line at customer service waiting to learn my options. After about thirty minutes, I walked to the airport terminal parking where he'd been waiting, furious.

"I spoke to Continental," I said to H. quietly. "The next flight to Cleveland is sold out and the only one I can get a seat on isn't until tomorrow morning."

My fiancé's bachelor party was scheduled for that night in Virginia Beach. Most of his friends couldn't afford to make the trip to Cleveland for our wedding, so they planned it for that night in town. He was so mad at me, it was like I could see anger steaming off of his face, like smoke emanating from hot pavement after a rain shower.

"But," I continued, a little less steady this time, "there's a flight leaving out of BWI in a few hours that has room for me."

Baltimore-Washington International airport was about four hours from where we lived. I knew that we could make the trip and he'd get back to Virginia just in time for his party. He knew it too, and without saying a word, he got out of the car and grabbed my suitcase, throwing it into the trunk of his car.

It was a long, silent drive. And when I say it was silent, I mean exactly that—he did not speak to me the entire four-hour drive. The only sounds I heard were the radio, the voice of my mom every time she called to see how the drive was going, and the squeal of worn car brakes that needed new pads, each time he slammed on them to emphasize his annoyance with me.

"How's the weather?" my mom asked during one of her calls.

"It's raining," I said. We'd driven through two thunderstorms so far, each one making H. visibly angrier.

"Well, you guys be careful, and tell my son that I love him."

"Mom said she loves you," I repeated to my fiancé once I'd hung up the phone. He said nothing.

And she did love him, as did my dad. My older brother is a quiet, introverted, skilled church pianist, and, somehow, I'd found his life twin to marry: a quiet, introverted, skilled church pianist. Those basic identical traits between my fiancé and my brother undoubtedly drew my parents to him. It was easy to love my fiancé because it was easy to love their son, my brother. My fiancé was an extra son, gelling so well with our dynastic makeup that it seemed like he'd been designed especially for the Gooden family.

When we pulled into the BWI airport terminal parking, I thought I'd escaped being hit; if silence was my punishment for inconveniencing him, then that was progress.

"We made it!" I sing-songed, mostly excited to get out of the car rather than the fact that we'd reached our destination.

"I'll get your bag."

He popped the trunk open, and I grabbed my purse and headed to the back of the car.

"Thank you for bringing me here, babe."

"You are so stupid," he replied as he put my suitcase on the ground.

There it was. It took four hours, but there was the person I knew.

I felt confident to argue with him because we were in public. We were parked close to the airport entrance, and a steady flow of travelers were walking by. I could say what I had to in the safety of public view and with forty-eight hours between this moment and the next time we saw each other, which might cool him down.

"I'm not stupid; it was an accident," I shot back, grabbing my suitcase handle.

"No, you're stupid and selfish. Why didn't you just pack?"

"I don't know, but we're here now, so it doesn't make sense to fight about it—that's what's really stupid."

I think it was the "really" that did it.

He reached for the handle of my suitcase and pulled it from me, twisting my thumb in the process.

"Stop!" I yelled, hoping someone would repeat after me and say it to him.

"You callin' me stupid after I drove you all the way to fucking Baltimore?"

This was escalating. I needed to get away. I tried to grab my suitcase back and get ahold of the handle, but he pushed me hard against the car, scrapping for control of the suitcase.

In the struggle, I could see travelers looking at us, though not one of them said anything. Not one of them stopped to help; each person looked and kept walking. There were at minimum ten people walking by. I now wonder what my eyes said as I made eye contact with a few of them. Did my eyes tattletale the panic I felt in that moment? Could they see the shame or embarrassment? I could see shame in *their* eyes, the result of a self-deception that convinced them that this wasn't their business. And maybe a little fear. But neither of those would help me.

I managed to push him off me and start running with my suitcase, my purse dangling from my arm. I ran all the way through the terminal. I didn't stop to look back, and travelers who had witnessed everything moved to the side while I ran, making a path for my getaway. A pathetic nod to the violence they'd ignored, but bore witness to, that afternoon.

Almost as soon as I made it to security, my phone rang. It was my dad.

"Hey, baby, did you make it?"

"Yes."

"Good, he must have done some good driving!"

"Yeah, he did real good, Daddy."

I could never quite bring myself to tell my parents what had been going on. I thought: *If I tell them what's going on, they'll hate him. And I can't have them hate him because he's definitely going to change. And even when he changes—because he's definitely going to change—they'll still hate him because of what he's done. It'd be better for me not to mention that sometimes he chokes me, or bites me, or slams my head against car windows. Because the most important thing is that my parents don't hate him because I don't hate him. I love him.*

So, as I stood there arm-in-arm with my dad before walking down the aisle to marry my fiancé, I was sure.

"Good, because we already paid for the food," my dad laughed.

My dad is a sugar-sweet, kindhearted, temperate man with the greatest smile and a loud laugh. The kind of man I wanted to marry. The kind of man I wanted to fashion my fiancé into being, even though all signs pointed to him being the opposite.

My dad loved him, and he trusted him. My mom adored him. I couldn't tell them because I had to protect them. My parents knowing what my fiancé did to me would have been an indictment on their ability to foresee danger for their child, an ability that every parent believes they innately hold. And this is part of the trouble of living through abuse: You try to protect everyone else, even as you fight for your own life.

When I did finally tell them in the fall of 2010, my mother's initial "oh no" was followed by a long silence, then crying. I cried too, mostly because I'd convinced myself this reveal would let them down. I'd heard them say, "I know they know better than that!" about people in our lives who'd gotten themselves into some kind of trouble or another, and I'd anticipated they'd say the same about me. But now I was planning to leave my husband, so they had to know. I wanted them to know exactly where I was; I didn't want my absence from the home they thought I lived in to be a surprise if they ever called looking for me.

I told them over the phone, because I was still living with H. in Texas, a thousand miles away from the safety of their presence.

"I know why you didn't tell us," my mom eventually said. "I understand."

I didn't interrogate that, maybe because the weight of the moment was too great. To me, it didn't matter. What did matter is that she wasn't using words like "crazy" or "know better." She was using words of compassion. For all our standard mother-daughter disagreements over the course of my life, and we had many, those words that day were like a balm on a wound that had been hidden, slowly rotting away.

All my dad could say in the moment was, "I love you, baby," but that was enough for me that day. I told them I loved them, that I'd stay in close contact while I planned next steps, and that if I ever disappeared or didn't respond for days, to assume the worst and call for help. Part of my plan to get out was to make clear to my family that I was fighting to live, not to die. And that if death came for me, it was not my choice.

My parents were the only people I could contact without raising the suspicion of my husband. And while I recognize that it hurt them to know what was going on, getting out of that house required them to know—not because they could help me get out, but because the secret of abuse now had a light on it. And in the worst-case scenario, that light could help lead to justice. A justice I might not be alive to see but would nonetheless bring peace to those who loved me.

In 2014, when *TMZ* released the video of former Baltimore Ravens running back Ray Rice punching his then-fiancée unconscious and dragging her out of an elevator, the internet exploded with questions about her. Why didn't she leave? Why did she marry him? Why did she stay? Their implied judgment, which should have been directed at her husband, made me sick. And while I could not speak for Janay Rice, I could speak for myself.

I created a Twitter hashtag, #WhyIStayed, and shared my reasons for staying in an abusive relationship. And I created the hashtag to de-scandalize "staying" and recognize that it is a coherent, reasonable choice when there are few, and to help other survivors of abuse *surrender the shame of that choice*. My only intention once it went viral was to educate and inspire, to inform others why I made that decision, and to show victims that there is life after abuse.

Then over 200,000 people unexpectedly joined me in sharing. This was not by request; I did not set out to start a movement, and I wouldn't have ever asked survivors to publicly bare their pain. But so many did, and it changed my life. Since then, I've traveled across the country to speak about my experiences and listen to the stories of people who also stayed. The more they shared, the more I realized that beyond the validation and empathy that the #WhyIStayed hashtag brought them, many wanted to know exactly how they could leave. They sought answers—and hoped that they could find those answers in the presence of survivors who made it out. Since then, it has been my mission to give survivors the tools and inspiration they need to get free and build a life of safety and independence.

I knew that reclaiming a life for myself would not be easy. Nothing about surviving abuse ever is. But the moment I made the choice to leave was the moment I embraced my *basic human right* to exist in a state of freedom, security, and happiness. And that's what we all deserve.

Chapter 3

WHY WE STAY

This chapter is about why I, and millions of others, stay in abusive relationships and how a relationship can begin beautifully and yet devolve, whether physically or nonphysically. The quirks that you soon realize are manipulative. The jokes that become not jokes, but verbal abuse. The "you look good in that" comments that gradually become, "Why are you wearing that?" And why we can't *just leave*.

A lot of time has passed since September 8, 2014, when I first tweeted #WhyIStayed. Much scholarship and research have been done, and I'm thankful to the students, activists, journalists, and academics who thought it necessary to dig deeper into the complexities of abuse. There have been many articles written, media commentators speaking about the hashtag and its effects on activism and public understanding of domestic violence, but I want to take you back to that day just to walk through it from the beginning.

The temporary job I was able to secure after leaving H. was in entry-level human resources at a tech company. I did not want to be in human resources, but I couldn't find a different role. I am control-averse; I don't like having say or power over the destinies of others, particularly in such a sensitive area of life as work and pay. To have influence is a positive, gratifying place for me as it leaves so much room for collaboration, but *control*—handing out disciplinary actions, making firm decisions about individual pay, enforcing strict attendance rules—is unpleasant to me. And human resources has a lot of that inherently as a function. Employment paths can be narrow in that, once you perform one function, your next job is in that same function. I tried to change career paths several times, even within the people function—I had an interest in organizational design—but to eat, I had to work. And the work that I repeatedly found was as a human resources (HR) generalist.

After my temp job ended at that company, I got another entry-level temp job in HR, then I moved into an HR associate level role, and then to an HR generalist role. Since it seemed I would be in the field awhile, I decided to give it my all, and I was good at it; I've always been good at connecting with people because of my curiosity. And because I viewed most things through the lens of social justice, I thought that I could advocate for employees at my company in areas such as pay equity and sexual harassment, like doing social justice within a corporate framework. So, I tried doing that for a long time, and after moving on from that company, I became an employee relations consultant, almost 100 percent focused on investigating cases of sexual harassment. I wrote sexual harassment policies and collaborated with companies to create pieces of training on appropriate workplace conduct, for example, keeping your hands and sexual innuendo to yourself. And it felt good to help others; after surviving abuse, it was fulfilling to be in a position to help make life safe for vulnerable people.

At the time of #WhyIStayed, I worked at a recreation facility in North Carolina as a human resources manager. Because I was an HR department of one, stress was high. During summers, an influx of part-time employees, mainly in the form of college students who were on break for the summer, joined the organization for two months. By September, they were returning to their college campuses, so I had a little bit more time on my hands to decompress, evaluate how our summer program worked for the students that year, and catch up with the coworkers nearby.

On that day, September 8, 2014, it was nearing my lunch break, and I usually checked Twitter before my lunch break back then to see what was going on. Twitter moves so fast that if you spend too much time away from it, when you do finally come back you'll have no idea what's going on.

The irony of all of this is that I wouldn't consider myself "good at" social media. I'm there now because as a writer, I'm supposed to be. But I barely post on Instagram, rarely visit Facebook, and have only written a handful of Twitter threads. And this tracks with my youth; I was not a popular or social kid. I wasn't teased or bullied, either. I was just sort of . . . there. In fact, I spent a lot of time awkwardly trying to fit in with others—a pursuit I've long given up on. My kindergarten teacher wrote a note to my parents one time that read: "Beverly is friendly, warm, and will play with any child who initiates play. But it seems she would much rather watch others play or play alone."

As I got older, I began to recognize the importance of social groups. Much more than networking, social groups can be havens and life sources. I've been invited into or created a few tight, intimate friend groups but when it comes to public spaces or large groups, I revert to the kindergartner who prefers to watch others play. On social media, this translates to a non-rhythmic posting schedule. And for years I was critical of my inability to consistently post content, particularly after going viral.

But as a person, I'm reserved but not timid; quiet but not hiding. I keep most things close to my chest. Deep curiosity often compels me to assume the role of silent observer, but when it is time to speak, I can do that with ease. And on that day, it was time to speak.

Now, I usually tweeted about the mundane, like music, my morning coffee, or my partner at the time. Whatever silly thing was going on in my life. But on this day, I saw something different once I logged on.

The gossip site *TMZ* released a video of then–NFL player Ray Rice punching his fiancée in the face and dragging her out of an elevator. I only knew that because I read tweets about the video; I did not watch it myself. As soon as I knew what happened in the video, I decided not to watch it. Instead, I watched everyone else's reactions to it.

And this was typical behavior for me. I've *never* wanted to see other people, particularly other women, experience physical violence. That's not something that I consider myself able to witness. I hide my eyes during fight scenes in movies. While this wasn't the first incident of intimate partner violence circulating on social media, it was the first I can remember that brought so much attention so quickly.

For a few minutes, the conversation revolved around the shock of witnessing a professional athlete act violently off the field and to their romantic partner. And it's not that we didn't know things like this happen; it's that this one was caught on surveillance video. It was in your face, circulating so widely on Twitter that it became practically unavoidable. Either you clicked on the video to watch it play out, or like me, you just kept scrolling quickly, trying to avoid that moment of impact.

But just as quickly as the conversation about violence against women began, it shifted; it became less about what he did to her and more about why she would *stay* with him. In my opinion, the shift resulted from tweets announcing that Ray Rice and his then-fiancée were now married.

And I could feel it coming. I could feel that tide turning because it has always been like this for as long as I can remember, in the time that I've been closely paying attention to the issue of domestic violence. While I was the first person to hashtag the words #WhyI-Stayed, I was not the first person to voice those reasons or push back against that question. Survivors, victims, womanists, feminists, researchers, academics, grandmothers, coworkers, friends—they all have, throughout history, begged people to stop asking the question, *why would they stay?*

But in that moment, when the jokes and rude comments started pouring onto my timeline, primarily via retweet, I began to feel a familiar shame—not necessarily the shame of experiencing an abusive relationship, although that is a toxic shame that some survivors carry, but the shame of experiencing abuse and *staying* with the person who did it. The scandal is in the *staying*.

I endured many years of toxic shame, and later in this chapter, I'll talk about how I moved through it. But in this moment, shame became a sticking point; it was overwhelming to read so many people pile on and degrade a person who had experienced violence in such a public way. And although the situation had nothing to do with me, and most of my followers didn't even know I'd been married much less experienced domestic violence, I felt targeted by that question—*Why would she stay with him?*

In a side discussion with Twitter friends, we started talking about how people misunderstand abuse survivors. At the time, I had about eight hundred followers on Twitter, mostly people I knew from college but some strangers that I'd grown close with over the three years I had been on Twitter.

The first person I saw pushing back against the question "Why did she stay with him?" was one of my mutual followers, Ricky Pulley Jr., a masculinities and antiviolence educator. He spent a few minutes retweeting survivors of domestic violence who were already sharing their stories of survival, some speaking of abuse dynamics, others criticizing blame directed at Janay Rice. I credit Pulley, in part, for the courage to speak about my experience that day; seeing someone I follow acting on behalf of survivors—not speaking over them or commenting on their stories, but simply sharing them—felt good.

I found an article about why victims stay with their abusers and tweeted it out using #WhyIStayed, which was my second use of it. My first use was in a tweet responding to a survivor that Pulley had retweeted. I wrote, "*I stayed because I thought it would get better. It never got any better. #WhyIStayed.*" And then, without really thinking about it, I started to tweet my reasons for staying:

> *I tried to leave the house once after an abusive episode, and he blocked me. He slept in front of the door that entire night.*
> *#WhyIStayed*

10:47 AM · September 8, 2014

I stayed because my pastor told me that God hates divorce. It didn't cross my mind that God might hate abuse, too. #WhyI-Stayed
10:48 AM · September 8, 2014

He said he would change. He promised it was the last time. I believed him. He lied. #WhyIStayed
10:51 AM · September 8, 2014

I had to plan my escape for months before I even had a place to go and money for the bus to get there. #WhyIStayed
10:52 AM · September 8, 2014

I stayed because I thought love was enough to conquer all. #WhyIStayed
10:53 AM · September 8, 2014

I stayed because I was halfway across the country, isolated from my friends and family. And there was no one to help me. #WhyIStayed
10:53 AM · September 8, 2014

And then, I locked my computer and went for a walk. The facility I worked at had beautiful trails and a whitewater rafting canal, so I often went on short walks if I felt frustrated. But my return to work that day was unlike any other day.

When I logged back onto my computer, Twitter was still on the screen. Twitter's user interface was much different than it is today; it was less confusing and laid out cleanly. There was an indicator of how many interactions you have on Twitter, like on your phone when you get notifications, and there was a little badge with numbers on it. Since I was an occasional tweeter back then, I usually had about seven or eight interactions a day. But that day, I had more than a hundred interactions.

I noticed that #WhyIStayed was among the topics slowly beginning to trend. At first, I was confused, thinking, "I wonder what
that's about?" Of course, I knew that I'd recently tweeted #WhyI-
Stayed, but I was not thinking that it could have anything to do with
me. People did not talk about domestic violence like that—not so
much that it would be a trending topic. And what was wild to me is
that #WhyIStayed was listed right beneath Ray Rice's name.

None of this was an indicator for me that anything was going on
with my #WhyIStayed, so much so that I ignored the trending topic
and moved on to see what technical error caused me to get a hun-
dred-plus interactions. But when I clicked to view the interactions, I
knew it was not a technical error. The #WhyIStayed that was trending was the #WhyIStayed that I created.

Survivors were tweeting their stories, primarily survivors sharing
reasons why they stayed. And it was incredible; there were reasons
that I would have never thought of. A user tweeted that she stayed
with her ex-husband because she lived with a chronic health condition and staying with him was the only way she could keep access to
the health insurance that provided her care. Another user tweeted
that she stayed because her "word was the only evidence" of abuse.

I witnessed queer survivors share their unique experiences. Non-
binary survivors, of which there are few statistics regarding abuse,
also spoke up. Trans women and men told of the types of abuse they
experience at home and in the world. I watched immigrants write
about hiding abuse out of fear of deportation and survivors with
mobility disabilities speak of how it was physically impossible to
get away.

And those things are important to me; they are essential for those
who have different lived identities. Whether you consider yourself
an "ally" or an "advocate," we can be neither of those things effectively without basic, functioning knowledge of how people different
than us experience abuse. #WhyIStayed demonstrated that while our
abuses may be similar, survivors are different in specific ways that
make the challenges of surviving very personal.

I began to think of writer Leslie Morgan Steiner who gave a
popular TED Talk[1] two years earlier in 2012 about why women stay

with men who have abused them—speaking directly to the issue of violence against women who are in relationships with men. In her TED Talk, she says:

> Why did I stay? The answer is easy. I didn't know he was abusing me. Even though he held those loaded guns to my head, pushed me downstairs, threatened to kill our dog, pulled the key out of the car ignition as I drove down the highway, poured coffee grinds on my head as I dressed for a job interview, I never once thought of myself as a battered wife. Instead, I was a very strong woman in love with a deeply troubled man, and I was the only person on Earth who could help Conor face his demons. The other question everybody asks is, why doesn't she just leave? Why didn't I walk out? I could have left any time. To me, this is the saddest and most painful question that people ask, because we victims know something you usually don't: It's incredibly dangerous to leave an abuser. Because the final step in the domestic violence pattern is kill her. Over 70 percent of domestic violence murders happen after the victim has ended the relationship, after she's gotten out, because then the abuser has nothing left to lose. Other outcomes include long-term stalking, even after the abuser remarries; denial of financial resources; and manipulation of the family court system to terrify the victim and her children, who are regularly forced by family court judges to spend unsupervised time with the man who beat their mother. And still we ask, why doesn't she just leave?

In short, I stayed because I loved him. At the time, I considered H. the love of my life, and I did not want to leave him. I wanted my baby back; I wanted the sweet, quiet, brooding guy who I fell for to come back to me. And I thought that was possible; I felt that if I just did the things that he wanted when he wanted, if I just behaved in the way he claimed he needed, that guy would come back to me. I wanted the violence to end, not the relationship.

I stayed because once we moved to Texas, I didn't have a support system. Anybody that I knew, I knew because of him. His coworkers and friends were my coworkers and my friends by proxy.

And I did not know them well enough to trust them with this secret that I carried.

Abuse *is* a secret. I stayed because I was keeping that secret, hoping that the details of that secret would one day die. By that, I mean I hoped that the abuse would end, never to be resurrected, and we could go on about our lives without this secret.

I stayed because I wanted to be every love song I'd ever heard about couples who go through challenges, stick together, and ultimately live a beautiful life. At the time, I didn't identify what I was experiencing as *domestic violence*; I wasn't versed in the language of abuse or its dynamics. I considered what was happening between us to be a "challenge," and I managed it as if it were a challenge, not as if it were an abusive relationship.

I stayed because I believed that divorce was unacceptable. I didn't think it was an option, and if it became an option, I didn't want to live with the perpetual shame I knew I'd feel walking into church every week after divorcing my husband.

The #WhyIStayed tweets kept spilling onto my Twitter timeline, and soon, victim-blaming tweets joined in the chorus. Sitting at my computer watching the topic unfold, I was *nauseous*. I felt a deep, twisted knot in my stomach while watching blowback on survivors sharing their stories. "I would NEVER let a man hit me!" some tweeted. "You are dumb for staying lol" was another frequent tweet. My heart was pounding, and my underarms wet; I felt responsible for whatever emotion that survivors receiving those tweets felt. I created this hashtag, and I felt horrible for survivors whose tweets were being met with shade, or worse, hostility. I'd already created several filters trying to mute hateful words, like "stupid" or "dumb." And I wished that I had a more prominent platform so that I could do more to fight back against bad actors attempting to distract from what #WhyIStayed was about. But all I could do was watch, jumping in to defend survivors as much as possible.

It didn't take long that day for people to start using #WhyIStayed in different ways—telling survivors they should "know their worth" and even going so far as to take credit for creating the hashtag. In a panic, and with the scent of *erasure* in the air, I sent a DM to Dr. Anthea Butler, associate professor of religious studies and Africana studies at the University of Pennsylvania, who I'd been following for a while. She'd started conversations on Twitter before about making sure women receive credit for the work they do on and offline, and regularly spoke about erasure of Black women in academia. I thought she may have some advice for when it happens on social media, too.

"Hi Dr. Butler," I wrote. "I hope you are well. I have a question. I started the #WhyIStayed hashtag, but folks are taking it over. Is there a way to control that? I just don't want folks using it with ill intention."

"The way to make sure you get credit is blog someplace about it RIGHT NOW," she replied. "Step all over it. Make sure you say you started it. When you put it up, send me a link."

I immediately logged in to my blog and wrote a short, new post,[2] "Why I Created the Why I Stayed (#WhyIStayed) Movement."

September 8, 2014

For over a year, I was physically abused by my ex-husband. When TMZ released the video of Ray Rice punching, dragging, and spitting on his wife this morning, the internet exploded with questions about her. Why didn't she leave? Why did she marry him? Why did she stay?

I can't speak for Janay Rice, but I can speak for Beverly Gooden. Why did I stay? Check out some of my reasons here. Leaving was a process, not an event. And sometimes it takes a while to navigate through the process.

I believe in storytelling. I believe in the power of shared experience. I believe that we find strength in community. That is why I created this hashtag. I hope those tweeting using #WhyIStayed find a voice, find love, find compassion, and find hope.

After tweeting the link and sharing it with Dr. Butler and a few other mutual followers, I crossed my fingers and prayed that someone would notice this post amid endless #WhyIStayed tweets. And to my surprise, many people did. People with the platforms that I did not have. People who invited me to talk about #WhyIStayed and its purpose on those platforms. The day after #WhyIStayed went viral, I was invited on *Good Morning America* to be interviewed by Robin Roberts. Flying to New York City for the interview was surreal; I never thought that a hashtag would propel me to a national news program studio, but I took that moment seriously. I was not nervous because I knew I was telling the truth. But the issue with going viral, particularly for situations such as abuse or sexual violence, is that there is always someone on the other side of your story, someone on the receiving end of an accusation.

I lived in Charlotte, North Carolina, at the time, and a local newspaper reporter had been following the hashtag on Twitter. It was evening when I got his email asking for an interview. "Sure," I wrote back, and gave him my personal cell phone number.

The next morning, I got a call from the reporter. We spoke for about thirty minutes—walking through why I created the hashtag, talking about the issue of domestic violence itself, and speaking briefly about my personal story. We were wrapping up the call when he said, "I understand you work at the Olympic training facility. How long have you been there?"

"About a year," I responded. "Why?"

"Oh, I'm going to put that in the article," he said.

I gasped. He was going to do what?

"No, I'm sorry but you can't do that."

"I have to do that," he said. "That's part of the story."

"Where I work is not part of the story," I replied. "*Where* I work has nothing to do with the story."

"Of course, it does," he said, condescendingly. "Everything about you is part of the story."

I felt lightheaded. If he wrote my place of employment, the only type of facility like that in the area, then H. would know where I worked. And if H. knew where I worked, he could show up. A survivor's worst fear is being found by the person who abused them, even if there has been no threat of violence recently.

I started to shake and cry.

"If you say where I work my ex-husband will know." I'd decided to spell it out for him. "And if he knows, I could be in danger."

"Well, aren't you in danger all the time anyway?" he asked, flippantly. "He could easily find out where you work some other way. Everything is public these days."

"No," I said. "I've been very careful not to give too many details about myself." Now I was mad. "Why is this so hard for you to understand?"

He started to respond, but I'd had enough. I didn't want to hear his response.

"Cut the story," I said.

"What?" he responded. "No, I can't do that . . ."

"Cut the story!"

I was screaming now, my once-calm voice now shrill and panicked.

He began stumbling over his words, part apology and part pleading. I said I was hanging up and that he did not have my permission to run the story. Shortly after hanging up the phone, I received an email from him, with his editor attached.

"Ms. Gooden," he began. He went on to explain that he understood what I must be going through with the attention, and that it must be difficult to have my story in public. But would I please speak on the phone to his editor, to talk through the story a bit more, to come to an agreement between us?

I wrote a quick, two sentence reply. "No, I am not interested in speaking with your editor, and you do not have my permission to publish my story. I can connect you with other survivors who may be willing to share their story with you, if you want."

What he did not understand is that I wasn't "going through" anything because of the attention, I was going through something because he failed to listen to me. And isn't that the story of so many victims of abuse? Here we are, telling the world exactly what we need, and the world is insistent on ignoring us. This reporter, pushing his agenda at the expense of my safety, made me feel exposed and afraid, just as I'd felt the day I left H.

I weighed whether to cancel the appearance on *Good Morning America*. The virality, I felt, had gotten out of hand. I did not want to talk about myself anymore, didn't want to be more exposed. I had no clue where H. was or if he knew what was going on. If he did know, what if he got angry and retaliated? What if he *did* find my personal info or home address and show up? This was the first moment since the hashtag took off that I felt powerless. It seemed no one wanted to protect me except me, and that made me think of, remember, and *feel* the experiences I had before I left my marriage.

I decided to go to New York, but while on the plane, I also decided that I wanted to speak less about myself, and more about the issue of victim-blaming at the heart of the question *"Why do they stay?"* I wanted to tell stories of survivorship. I wanted attention to be on those who abuse their partners, whether physically, emotionally, verbally, psychologically, or financially. I didn't want to be a voice for all victims and survivors, because I can't be that. I can only be my voice. But I wanted to clear a path at that moment, even if that moment only lasted a week or two. I hoped that the path would help others become comfortable with their own story, their own voice, and have that voice taken seriously. Even though I was more scared, cautious, and guarded after the incident with the reporter, I wanted to get on that stage and share both the pain and joy of surviving abuse.

I also wanted to prove that there is knowledge outside of established power structures, that survivors in the margins had something to say. Back then, those who were interviewed about domestic violence worked professionally in the domestic violence field itself, for instance, the CEO of the National Network to End Domestic Violence or leaders at the YWCA. Very few interviews or national campaigns included individual survivors, and when they did, the goal was to highlight their trauma for awareness.

After I left Texas, I returned to grad school in Chicago at the urging of the program's director, and earned my master's degree in social justice that fall, completing the nine remaining credits I had left and writing my thesis on institutional responses to domestic violence survivors. That in hand, I applied for jobs at domestic violence agencies, big and small. Often, I received no response, and when I did, they were denials. Rejection after rejection, I felt unwelcomed in the movement and unfit to even *work* in it.

But #WhyIStayed was a great equalizer; a few tweets placed many survivors on a high-speed train, zooming past the structures that either outright ignored us or said, "wait your turn." Survivors who participated in #WhyIStayed went on to become advocates and influencers on different platforms like Instagram; some create domestic violence prevention content on TikTok. Others, like me, spend time traveling to colleges and other events, speaking about surviving abuse and chasing after healing. Many focus their attention locally, founding groups that help victims of abuse in their hometowns.

I returned home from the *Good Morning America* appearance, and after a few weeks, things began to slow down. The attention on me faded, and the issue of domestic violence lost popularity. With more time to think on my hands, I wanted to do something other than just talk. I really wanted to act in a tangible way, to create something that would have a substantial effect on survivors—something measurable.

I thought, what was one of the hardest parts of leaving abuse? Aside from managing difficult emotions, what was plain difficult or burdensome?

The escape bag.

In the next chapter, I'll go into detail about how I left my marriage. But in short, part of my leaving was carefully constructing an escape bag of toiletries and clothing, then hiding it in my closet. So, I decided to create what I call the Bolt Bag project—"bolt" as in "running out of the door," an idea born from my own experience of making that bag. With my Bolt Bags, none of that is necessary as I create the bag for victims and send it wherever they want, be it a job or a friend's apartment.

When I started traveling for speaking engagements, I noticed that hotels would leave a few of each toiletry—soap, lotion, shampoo—

in each room, regardless of occupancy number. I began bringing my toiletries and collecting what was in the hotel room as soon as I arrived. If I stayed more than one night and the housekeeper refreshed the room, I'd stash the replacements in my suitcase too. Then, I'd take them home and use the stash to assemble escape bags for victims of abuse. If I needed any items that hotels did not provide, such as toothbrushes, toothpaste, and hand sanitizer, I would buy them myself. The project is entirely anonymous; victims can give an alias to avoid using their real name, and all address records are erased each evening. There is no contact, no expectation of sharing personal information with me, and no strings.

When #WhyIStayed first went viral, there were several spin-off hashtags, mainly because people wanted to relieve the pressure on survivors. The toughest criticism I heard of #WhyIStayed was that it asked survivors to explain themselves when they should not be expected to. And I understand that criticism; I agree that survivors should not carry the burden of defending their actions in the face of violence and that in most cases, undressing your wounds on social media does not lead to a safer or more just society. #WhyIStayed was not a planned, organized awareness effort designed to bend public opinion. I chose to tweet my reasons for staying, and other survivors joined me. And I'm thankful for their sacrifice because, in that moment, *I* felt less afraid and ashamed.

Still, I hope that the survivors who participated in #WhyIStayed did not feel any pressure to, or that it was required of them to provide validation of their experience. I hope that all participation provided momentary, if not lasting, relief from our private nightmares since we know that attaining the traditional idea of "justice" is unlikely for us. In that moment, we were our own justice; our togetherness was a balm. #WhyIStayed was not about exposing ourselves or proving our worth to others; #WhyIStayed was about community and comfort.

Of note though, is just how right Dr. Butler was about crediting yourself for the things you create. In the years that have passed since that day, I've watched myself be repeatedly erased from the hashtag. If not for close friends who push back, and those who worked to create a Wikipedia page for #WhyIStayed, I fear that I would have long been removed from the record.

One thing I love about the story behind the 2017 creation of the #MeToo hashtag is that Tarana Burke, knowing she'd spent years building the #MeToo movement, also knew that her work could be overlooked, or its meaning *altered* in that moment. She reached out to her network of friends for help getting the word out that "me too" already existed. And Alyssa Milano—the incredibly famous, powerful woman who started using the hashtag that day—responded not only by giving Tarana credit but also by making room on massive platforms for Tarana, a Black woman, to be seen.

It has been the opposite for me and for many Black women who came before me.

Everything is cyclical, particularly when it comes to social media. #WhyIStayed happened in 2014, which by now is long enough for platforms to have cycled through old and new users. Many who participated in #WhyIStayed don't use Twitter anymore, and newer users weren't around for that day. So much has happened since then as well—the transition from a Democratic U.S. president to the 2016 Donald Trump presidency, for example, which created a new generation of activists speaking out on social causes like violence against women and child sexual abuse.

Some would say *who* started a hashtag or movement doesn't matter. But as a person who started one, erasure is so painful; it's a feeling of being buried alive. During the early Trump presidency's gender activism surge, a high-profile survivor of domestic violence went viral for a moving blog post titled "Why I Stayed," one that I shared with others. But then, #WhyIStayed trended again on social media. I watched as a cable news show had the survivor on, a White woman, speaking about why she created #WhyIStayed. Which was a record-scratch moment, since I appeared on that exact same show a few years earlier discussing the creation of #WhyIStayed with the exact same host. I'm not embarrassed to say that I cried about it; it is a heartbreaking thing. Like when a colleague takes or *is given* credit for work that you did, or an idea that you conceived of.

The cable news show eventually tweeted a correction after being called out by some of my friends. The survivor did not, but she quickly switched to using a different hashtag that includes the words "I stayed." But by then it was far too late. Users on the big three social media platforms, news outlets, podcasts, and other websites had already attributed credit for my work to someone else—and there was nothing I could do about it.

It is so easy to disappear Black women, to write them out of history, whether the contribution was large or small. We're having discussions these days about how society responds to White women in ways it does not respond to women of color. I will always fight to claim and reclaim my words, even though it's exhausting. I'll fight to be recognized because of what I've given up since that day. And I fight to honor the survivors who were a part of that moment because of what they sacrificed that day, too.

In a 2014 interview, I spoke of how #WhyIStayed helped change the conversation about domestic violence. And while that is enough for some, I want more. I want safety for survivors, and I want economic justice. I want upward financial mobility for anyone who has lived through intimate partner violence, and I want better, more inclusive laws that explicitly protect them. There are limits to what "changing" or "starting" a conversation can do. Conversation can inform, inspire, and educate. But conversation alone does not solve social issues. *Action does.*

After taking time to decompress, I started to evaluate how the #WhyIStayed disclosures might help me better connect with other survivors as I started traveling around to meet with them.

THREE REASONS WHY WE STAY

The main thing I wanted to do was figure out the commonalities between survivors. While our reasons are many, our similarities are what link us together. And here is what I found: The top three reasons why victims stay, according to what I understood examining the hashtag response, are dependence, fear or threats, and love.

Dependence

For half of our relationship, I was financially dependent on H. Be it
by design or by necessity, I needed H. to provide the basics for me.
That is the story of many abuse victims; we are either partially or
wholly dependent on the abusive person. Sometimes it is not financial dependence. It could be emotional or economic. According to a
research study titled "The Complex Relationship Between Dependency and Domestic Violence: Converging Psychological Factors
and Social Forces," by Robert Bornstein,[3] dependence goes both
ways; victim dependency and perpetrator dependency play a role in
why victims stay in abusive relationship. Victims may be economically dependent or emotionally dependent, although Bornstein
writes that for women specifically, emotional dependence is a less
likely reason for staying. But a victim's economic dependence coupled with the abusive partner's emotional dependence on the victim,
including depending on a partner to behave a certain way in order
for them to feel in control or at peace, creates a dynamic where the
victim depends on the abuser for day-to-day living, thus sacrificing
safety in order to keep the abuser emotionally stable.

Of that complex interdependence, Bornstein writes, "Research
confirms that dependency plays a significant role in domestic violence: High levels of economic dependency in a woman and high
levels of emotional dependency in a man independently predict the
likelihood that the woman will be physically abused by her partner.
Moreover, women's economic dependency is also associated with a
decreased likelihood of terminating an abusive relationship." He
further says that there is data to suggest that physical abuse occurs at
the *same frequency* within gay and lesbian relationships as it does in
the straight population.

Fear/Threats

Actress Sarah Hyland, most known for her character "Haley" on the
TV show *Modern Family*, was secretly in an abusive relationship
for years. Following the breakup and subsequent court filings for a

restraining order, Hyland wrote of her ex-boyfriend, "[He] relentlessly bombarded me with vile, threatening and emotionally disturbing texts and voice mails including his own suicide threats."[4]

I can't begin to describe how frightening it is to be with someone who is unpredictably violent. Every sudden movement, every comment, every threat must be taken seriously. We already know that person is capable of violent behavior, so why wouldn't we believe them if they give us a direct threat? Some abusive partners say things like, "If you leave me, I'll kill myself," or "If you tell anyone, you'll regret it." Victims of abuse often choose to take all threats seriously because you never know which threat might become real *action*.

Love

By now, you know that I loved H. and believed that in the end we would be okay. That is also the story of many survivors; we trust the person we love to *love* us, not abuse us. And if other victims are like me, we hold on to a great hope—a wishful expectation that love will prevail. When I left H., I loved him deeply. And after I had been gone, I still loved him deeply.

The love that ties other survivors together is love for children and family. A desire to preserve that structure. Many think it's in a child's best interest to have both parents present in the home, especially if the abusive partner has never hurt the children. And this is compelling; it's widely considered true that children want both parents—if a second parent was ever involved in the first place—to be a part of their daily life. But in the last few years I've watched as more information is released about the negative effects just *witnessing* abuse has on children.

Love was a reason I chose to stay with him, and now I was choosing to ignore the love I felt for him to leave. I'm a child of solid gold soul music; the classic hits from Black artists of the sixties and seventies (blame my parents). That said, all I remember about love songs is that love is supposed to be *unconditional*. Artists frequently crooned about "staying together" or "come back to me," "I'm nothing without you," or even the classic, "I ain't goin nowhere!" Healthy lines, like "Let's stay together if you want, and also if we treat each other with kindness and respect," never seemed to make it into the love songs.

So, I had to tell myself new things about love. In a world that pushes the concept of unconditional love, I told myself that love has conditions, and a lack of abuse is one of them. Believing that love alone could conquer all, I told myself that love could not conquer this, that only he could conquer his behavior, and he chose not to do that. Thinking that love of others was more important than loving me, I told myself that my greatest love, the most precious love I'll ever experience, is self-love. I had to reorient my mind and heart; I had to create different principles of love—its purpose, cost, and promise.

VICTIM BLAMING

The reason I talk about victim-blaming so much is that I think it has become routine, societally. Victim blaming is so normalized, so *accepted*, that it could be considered a valid critique of any situation with any amount of complexity, big or small. And in my experience, victim-blaming happens particularly to women; it is the natural reaction to instances of violence or abuse.

Victim blaming, at its core, is a tactic, a tactic used by the abusive person to escape responsibility and a tactic used by society to neutralize accountability. In the case of physical abuse, when the abusive person victim blames, they may say things like "If you didn't do _____, I wouldn't have hit you." When it's societal, regardless of abuse type, you may hear things like "Well, you knew they had a bad temper, so you shouldn't have disagreed with them in the first place."

So why do people victim blame? Optimism and cognitive bias.

Have you ever heard someone say, "That could never happen to me"? As a survivor, I've heard people say, "I would never let anyone hurt me!" Optimism bias, in this context, is when those who have not experienced abuse convince themselves that abuse is not something they *could* experience, for reasons they also create themselves. One reason might be that they are "too smart" or "will always leave a bad relationship." Optimism bias transforms into victim-blaming when we begin to attribute blame based on those reasons we've created, that is, you experienced abuse because you are *not* smart enough to see the signs.

In 1980, social psychologist Melvin Lerner published *The Belief in a Just World: A Fundamental Delusion*, in which he describes his theory, the just-world hypothesis. The just-world hypothesis is the idea that the world functions in a morally fair and appropriate way and any undesirable circumstance is a consequence of someone's personal actions. This theory is rooted in the belief that one can move through the world in a predictable way. This leads to behaviors or words that blame the individual rather than the situation or institution.

It is easier to view a victim as blameworthy than to let go of the belief that the world is fair and that everyone ultimately gets what they deserve. Because if we let that go, we must also accept that the world is frightening, dangerous, and unjust. If bad things happen to good people, it means that we too could be *vulnerable to abuse*, that no one is exempt. The good news is that we can both accept that the world is unjust while believing that we can make the world a more just place. I'll go into more details about that in a later chapter.

By victim blaming, *we perpetuate abuse*. I want you to remember that abusers want people to victim blame. Because the more we blame victims the less likely they are to report being victimized, and that allows abusers to continue abusing.

ENDING TOXIC SHAME

The one feeling that did not fade out over time was shame.

About two years after I left, I developed generalized anxiety and an eating disorder and needed medication for both. When asked by my doctor why I felt these problems were emerging, I couldn't say; I attributed them to the stress-filled process of rebuilding my life.

But it was much deeper than that.

Shame is that feeling that most often accompanies an admission of guilt. But *toxic* shame is not when you feel bad about what you did, but rather, you feel bad about *who you are.*

I told myself, *You subjected yourself to continual abuse and even confessed love for the person who abused you. How embarrassing. You make poor choices in life and love. You attracted an abuser and allowed him to be abusive for years. You are so stupid.*

That is toxic shame. And toxic shame will make it so that everything you do, even things you've always done well, like word processing at your day job or singing in the choir, seem wrong. Toxic shame is a breeding ground for imposter syndrome. "I don't deserve to be here," or "they should have picked someone else for this job," becomes a constant refrain because of toxic shame, and those feelings can hold you back from success. With toxic shame, you tell yourself that you can't do anything right because of this *one thing* that happened. You doubt your own opinions. You don't trust your own thoughts.

Toxic shame becomes a roadblock to healing as you tell yourself you don't *deserve* better. If you feel that way about yourself, I see you. And I hope these following words help you heal from it: *Trust yourself.* Trust your own story. Trust in the knowledge that you and *only you* are the expert of your situation.

It is challenging to defeat shame, and I wish I could tell you there was a shorter, more specific way to go about it. For me, there wasn't. I had to repeatedly tell myself that there was nothing to be ashamed of, over and over again until I *believed* that. The person who should feel shame about abuse is the abusive person. The only fault lies with the person who hurt you.

Defeating toxic shame took evaluating every area of my life and letting go of any person or thing, for example, a church or a friend, that made me feel bad. It will be impossible to defeat toxic shame if you are regularly told your experience was because of your own sin, or even karma. Let go of the things that ask you to attribute blame to yourself, people who contribute to your feelings of shame.

Engage counterpoints to the toxic shame. I deal with feelings of unworthiness in connection with how undeserving H. made me feel at times. Writing this book, I've said to myself, "What makes you think you can write this book? You're not special," and "No one is going to read this book." And when those thoughts creep up, I flip them. I'll say to myself, "Many people love to read what you write and you're *capable* of writing this book," and "This book will be read and deeply understood by millions of people." I work to defeat toxic shame by telling myself the opposite of what shame is saying to me. I separate myself from the toxic shame; I draw a clear line between what toxic shame is saying and what I choose to believe. And I choose to believe delightful things about myself now.

The final thing I recommend in defeating toxic shame is to be open with others about the way toxic shame impacts your mental and emotional wellbeing and to build a support system—strong relationships with one or two people who, when you're feeling that toxic shame, will remind you that you are *okay*. Better than okay! You're a survivor.

Some situations we find ourselves in are senseless, and we do the best we can to navigate them. There is no abuser-detector, no red-flag alert flashing like a traffic light above the head of people you meet, that 100 percent would have spared you from going through what you survived. And when these situations happen to us, we engage in meaning-making, that is, forming an interpretation of an event that then guides us in creating significance out of our situation. Because that significance helps us understand why painful things happen in the first place. But not all things require meaning; not all pain has a reason. And sitting in that space between "a terrible thing happened to me" and "there is no reason for it" can be uncomfortable, at best.

I choose not to assign reason or meaning to the abuse that I survived. It is something awful that happened, something that changed my life, and something that could happen to anyone. I did not go looking for abuse; I went looking for love. And in looking for love, abuse found me. And that abuse did not arrive leading with brutality; it arrived beautifully, pouring excitement and passion on my heart. A love so sweet that I could smell it. And when it turned sour, I could smell that too. It's just that my sour was different than other sours because of violence.

Reject any thought or assertion that attributes blame to you. You stayed? You have a right to stay; you rightfully have the expectation to exist in your home without your partner being violent. It is *your* home too! You thought they would change but they didn't, so it's your fault for believing them? It is normal for us to trust our partners not to hurt us. And if they choose to hurt us, no matter how many times they made that choice, your belief in them does not make *their* choice to fail you your fault. You got on your partner's nerves or did that thing they don't like? Your partner's boss gets on their nerves and does things your partner doesn't like *all the time*. You know this because your partner tells you about it. Ask yourself, does your partner also abuse their boss? Or do they only abuse you? If your partner can manage their anger at their boss, then they can also manage their anger at you.

You did not attract abuse; you did not invite abuse, were not destined to experience abuse, and were not at fault for the abuse *even if you stayed*. Someone else chose to be violent toward you, and that was a choice they made that only they are responsible for. Nothing about experiencing abuse or staying with someone abusive makes you stupid or less than. You made the best decision that you could with the information that you had at that time.

You are amazing.

Chapter 4

NO ONE IS GOING TO SAVE YOU

In the last chapter I wrote about the variety of reasons why we stay, but now I want to write about how we leave—the difficulties, the stressors, the challenges, and the solutions.

Lying in bed one night after a fight, and with H. in my arms, I remember thinking, *No one is going to save me. I'm going to have to save myself.* But how do you save yourself? Is it alright to save yourself? As I thought this through, I realized that I had two things working against me: I didn't have any money, and I'm a Black woman.

I learned about financial abuse in 2016 while working with the Allstate Foundation's Purple Purse initiative. Rather, I learned that financial abuse had a name. I earnestly thought that H. having control over our finances, including the decision of whether I could earn money, was his right as my husband—the "leader" of our home. The concept of a partnership where two people make those decisions together was not on my radar. Blame it on my religious childhood. Most of the marriages I saw growing up were designed this way; I didn't think that type of control could be harmful.

Financial abuse is when one person in a relationship uses money or financial tools to control their partner. This can mean withholding money, denying access to credit cards or money apps, taking out loans in a partner's name (even with their consent) if the intention is to achieve control, or forbidding a partner to have their own individual banking accounts—and this is only a summary of the ways abusive partners can use finances as a weapon. There are many more. Financial abuse is the most common form of abuse in relationships; it's one of the ties that bind all forms of relationship violence.

In fact, one study found that financial abuse occurs in 99 percent of violent relationships.[1] The purpose is to trap the target, to make it either impossible or considerably difficult for them to leave the relationship.

When activists talk about the importance of intersectionality when considering social issues, we mean this: Social identities and categorizations such as race, age, gender identity, class, citizenship status, and even language must always be considered, particularly in situations of violence, because these identities often overlap to create unique circumstances of oppression and discrimination.

I am Black. Not just Black, but a Black *woman*. And while Black women are expected to *do* the saving and rescuing,[2] it has been my observation that Black women don't *get* rescued.

When I started to think about leaving, it became clear how unachievable a goal that was, due to a lack of, well, anything related to money. A poor Black woman can't always walk into a bank and ask for a loan or a credit card and be taken seriously. Why? Structural racism.

Of structural racism, the Urban Institute writes, "The deep racial and ethnic inequities that exist today are a direct result of structural racism: the historical and contemporary policies, practices, and norms that create and maintain white supremacy."[3] Aspen Institute's Roundtable on Community Change defines structural racism as "a system in which public policies, institutional practices, cultural representations, and other norms work in various, often reinforcing ways to perpetuate racial group inequity."[4]

Structural racism is intentional; its very design is to exclude. It is a truly American feature, not the bug that many believe we can fix by making small policy changes. It *is* the policy. Structural racism is not something I was ever taught; it is simply something I have always lived. It is the reason why Black women die before, during, or after childbirth 2.5 times more often than White women,[5] with Harvard Public Health noting that when Black women complained of severe symptoms, "clinicians were more delayed and seemed to believe them less."[6]

Structural racism is the reason for the ever-growing racial wealth gap in the United States, where Black people hold less than 3 percent of America's total wealth,[7] having been segregated, discriminated against, and denied access to tools such as homeownership and professional advancement opportunities—or having been violently stripped of intracommunity efforts to build our own wealth structures, like when White mobs destroyed what was known as the Black Wall Street in Tulsa, Oklahoma.[8]

The combination of being Black and a woman is its own affliction. Moya Bailey coined the term *misogynoir* in 2010, a blending of the words "misogyny" and "noir"—the French word for black—to describe racism that is specific to Black women.

It is what Dr. Barbara Carroll felt in 2018 when trying to cash a $140 check at a Wells Fargo bank, the very bank from which the check was drawn.[9] After presenting the check and two forms of identification, the teller and bank manager withheld the money from her, threatening to call the police. Are we supposed to trust the vulnerable details of our safety to a system that refuses $140 of her own money to a Black woman?

In 2020, a homeowner decided to refinance her home, as interest rates decreased amid the COVID-19 pandemic.[10] Part of the home buying or selling process is what's known as an appraisal, an assessment that provides a bank with what *should be* an unbiased estimate of the value of a home. The homeowner, a Black woman, scheduled an appraisal, knowing that the value of other homes in her neighborhood were in the mid-$400,000s. However, the appraisal came back at $330,000. Knowing that this was inaccurate and understanding how the presence of a Black person historically undervalues real estate, she arranged for her husband, a White man, to be the sole person present for a second appraisal. That appraisal came back well above the initial expected value at $465,000, proving what Black people already know: The mere presence of our Black bodies depreciates worth.

And if our presence depreciates worth in *our own homes and neighborhoods*, just imagine the hurdles thrown in our paths when seeking financial help outside of our homes.

My own parents' finances have swung between lower middle class to low income, so them rescuing me, as much as they wanted to, was impossible. But I had to leave, because the chances of law enforcement launching a search for me if I came up missing were small. It is estimated that 64,000 to 75,000 Black women and girls are currently missing in the United States.[11] In my hometown of Cleveland, Ohio, Anthony Sowell, a serial killer now known as the Cleveland Strangler, murdered at least eleven Black women, whose bodies were found at his home. The families had been reporting these Black women missing to police *for years*, but no massive search or full investigation was launched.

Consider the response to racial justice activist Oluwatoyin Salau.

Oluwatoyin "Toyin" Salau was a Nigerian-American model, activist, and business owner, a native of Tallahassee, Florida. She was known for being vocal on Twitter about injustice in Tallahassee, and advocated for justice in the case of Tony McDade, a trans man killed by police officers in May 2020.[12]

After the cruel murder of George Floyd by police officer Derek Chauvin, Salau regularly attended protests against police violence in the Tallahassee area. At one of the protests, Salau recited the names of Black men and women killed by police, and said, "I don't want their names gone in vain."[13]

Then, on June 6, 2020, Salau disappeared after publicly tweeting that she had been sexually assaulted in Florida. Her Twitter thread was lucid and clear-eyed, explicitly stating where she had been and when. But there was no huge search for her. About a week later, she was found dead.

Only she wasn't found alone. The body of Victoria Sims was found alongside Salau's, murdered by the same man. Sims, a seventy-five-year-old White woman, had been reported missing *less than twenty-four hours earlier*, and the search for her began immediately. It could be surmised that in the search for Sims, Salau was accidentally discovered. Salau, a poor Black woman, was left to die alone. No one went to rescue Salau. For me, her words "I don't want their names gone in vain" indicate that she held a now haunting truth close to her—that the violent deaths of Black people, Black people who were not rescued from danger, Black people like herself, are rendered meaningless unless someone speaks up for them.

And no one came to rescue me. I saved myself.

One of the first questions survivors ask me about divorce is: "Did you hire a lawyer?"

Before we go there, let's establish one thing: Family law is complex. Complicated, even. But I did not hire an attorney. I represented myself. Domestic violence cases are personal and specific; no one case is identical to another. If you have the resources to hire an attorney, I suggest that you do. But if you are divorcing and you don't have those resources, I hope you find this part helpful.

I never intended to represent myself; it just happened. For one thing, I was poor (but, funny thing, not poor enough to qualify for court-fee waivers). Fortunately, I lived in a very "pro se" county. Pro se means do it yourself (DIY), so there were websites and forms to guide me along the way. However, the websites and forms only provided blanks to fill in, not legal advice. Since there was a significant amount of time between when I left, when I could afford to file, and when I could request a hearing, I had time to study a little family law.

The first thing I discovered is that family law is designed to provide protection for everyone. (Yes, that means the offender too.) This is one of the hardest things you, survivors who are reading this, will have to come to terms with. Family law works both ways, and it seems to be on the side of the person who has the evidence.

With that said, it's vital to strategize. *Think.* Stop, look, and listen. Get rational. Tactical. Purposeful. Now is the time to protect yourself and your future.

I did not have any children or own property with him. We weren't even officially married long enough to celebrate all the national holidays in a year. But I still had to be smart.

My strategy was twofold: Plan to get out of our home safely and prepare for life after leaving. A few days after the final violent incident, I did an internet search for advice on how to escape domestic violence. One of the first things that came up on almost every website was creating a safety plan, which included an escape bag. An escape bag can hold any items you feel necessary: medicine, toiletries, identification, money. My escape bag would include the basics—one set of clothes, a few toiletry items, and some cash.

Since I didn't have access to a bank account of my own, any money that I had was directly from H. giving me grocery money to shop with. I knew enough about him to know that he wouldn't notice if small amounts of money were gone. For instance, he didn't look at the receipts to make sure all the money was spent on grocery items. He just wasn't that meticulous.

I decided to use grocery money and buy items for my escape bag. Those items included deodorant, toothbrush, toothpaste, lotion, tampons, and a first aid kit, just in case I was injured when I tried to leave. And every time I was alone at the grocery store, I headed to the travel aisle to get one or two of these items. When I got back home, I made sure he wasn't looking and put those items in a bookbag I'd hidden on the floor of my side of the closet. He never went to my side, so he never noticed the bag.

Next, I wanted to preserve important documents and special items, because I knew that once I left that apartment, I'd never go back. Rifling through my things, trying to figure out what to take and what to leave, felt shitty—very shitty. What was the right amount to take before he noticed things were missing? Should I take family photos, or risk leaving them behind and not having those memories anymore? Should I take documents that belonged to the both of us? And what about the things he'd given me? Did I want to bring those things into my new life?

I felt sad and lost. Even though I was so clear on where I was going and why, it still felt like failure, like I was packing to walk away from a life that I couldn't figure out how to make work. I sat cross-legged on the floor of our closet, looking through our wedding photos. A part of me wanted to take them so that I could remember that day. But, if I was more honest with myself, it wasn't even really a happy day. I had happy moments, mostly because of my family. But it was a frightening day, a confusing day, a day I didn't really want to remember. So, I left them behind.

Even now, as I sit writing this, I think of how sad a time that was—just letting go. You might think it's easy to let go of a person who has terrorized you in any way, but it's hard to let go of a person in whom you can see the good, even in their worst moments when that goodness is undetectable.

I was never scared that he'd figure out what was going on be-cause I knew that details weren't his thing. He wouldn't notice if small things were missing, or if my things were missing. At times, I wasn't even sure if he would notice I was missing. Toward the end of our relationship, things became so weird between us; there was no violence, but there was also no resolution. It was an emotional purgatory that neither of us was really trying to escape. I just kept planning because one thing I was sure of was that he might hurt me at any moment. And I was done with that.

One afternoon, we were riding in the car, and I saw a sign that read "first month for $1!" at a storage facility. The next time that I had the car to myself, I cut the grocery trip short so that I could swing by the storage facility and get a unit. I didn't know how I would pay the $50 fee for the second month, but the most important thing to me was to ground myself in a place outside of my home. And that place was a storage unit—something that belonged to only me that he did not have access to.

So that became a pattern—cutting my grocery runs short to work my escape plan. He had a predictable schedule after work; since he was a musician, he spent a lot of time with headphones on, playing his keyboard and producing beats. I could grab things, put them in my big purse, and take them to the car before my grocery run, and he wouldn't notice. Over the course of a week, I got my passport, some books, my photo albums with pictures of family and friends, our marriage certificate in case I needed it for some reason, and copies of my driver's license into the storage unit.

While he was at work, I started to apply for jobs using an email address that I'd secretly created. I made sure to leave my cell phone number off of applications and just listed that secret email address. Even though I had plenty of professional experience, it was difficult to find a job due to my one-year break in employment after getting married.

My degree is in journalism and communications, but so many jobs listed qualifications I didn't have. *Three years reporting experience, advanced Microsoft Word user.* I applied to what felt like hundreds of jobs—journalism, reporting, public relations assistant, mailroom clerk at a newsroom, nonprofits—but nothing. I branched out and started applying for administrative roles—executive assistant, administrative assistant, office assistant, receptionist. Still nothing. I was a restaurant server in high school and thought I could fall back on that people skill at any time. Twenty or so server and host job applications later, I was still unemployed.

But I just kept trying, kept applying, and kept hoping. Hope is important when leaving an abusive relationship. Some days, applying to jobs was the only hope I had for a different life.

The hardest part of escaping was finding a place to live. I could not individually apply for an apartment without the leasing companies verifying all information possible. They would have to contact H. If not directly, they would do so indirectly by verifying bank accounts and past address history.

Our small apartment was across the street from the complex's leasing office. I'd applied for apartments before so I knew how it went, but I still wanted to verify the process.

"We'll need two recent paystubs, a driver's license, three months of bank statements, five years' rental history, four references, and a copy of your social security card."

"What if I don't have paystubs?" I asked the leasing manager.

"Then you'll need an offer letter from a job or one year of bank statements to show you have money to pay the rent."

I didn't have money to pay the rent. I didn't even have money to buy Doritos.

"And the application fee is $50. If you're approved, it's gonna be a one-month's rent security deposit, plus the first month's rent."

I didn't have that either. Was I going to have to go to a shelter? The irony of it all was that before I started dating H., I wrote federal grants for homeless shelters, which included domestic violence shelters. I knew the odds of me securing a spot were slim; many domestic violence shelters are reserved for families, specifically women with children. I was a woman, yes, but a woman without a family. It felt wrong to take up a kid's potential space.

But what else was I supposed to do? I couldn't stay. I *wouldn't* stay. I couldn't get home to Cleveland. I had no friends in the area to live with, and I had no money.

I went back to our apartment and just cried. Cried so hard my face was swollen. Cried so much I couldn't see anymore. Was I going to have to stay? Was this going to be another reason on the lengthy list of reasons why I stayed? I felt like I couldn't catch a break; no one would give me a break. I expected someone to help me, but I didn't know why—no one had even helped me in the airport parking lot.

To know there is no help coming for you, no savior, is to understand aloneness in the most desperate, heartsore way. I knew there was no easy way out of this marriage. But I had committed myself to getting out, by any means necessary.

Resigned that my only option was to go to a domestic violence shelter, I googled one in the area. I did not google two, or a few. I googled one. Pretending to be a donor, I called the agency to ask a few questions. I was hesitant to use my real name and disclose that I was living through domestic violence because I wasn't sure whether this would set off a required "intake" for me—I didn't know if the person who answered would be required to act. I could just see my husband and me sitting on the couch, watching the news or something, and a police officer knocking on the door because they "got a call" or "traced my phone."

"The Women's Shelter, how can I help you?" said a polite, but weary-sounding woman on the other end of the phone.

"My name is Beverly, and I have a few questions about your organization. I'm hoping you could answer them?" I couldn't tell if my statement was a question, but I felt awkward hearing it spill out of my mouth.

"Sure, what can I answer for you?"

"Is the shelter at this address?" I read the address that I'd found listed on the internet back to her.

"The location of our emergency shelter is confidential," she said matter-of-factly. There was a brief silence as I waited for her to go on. She did not.

"Oh . . . okay. Um, do you have stuff for people who need help, like food?" It was then that I realized I didn't know exactly what I wanted to know.

"Oh yes, we provide a range of services to our clients. We have food here at our office and our shelters have kitchens. We also offer help with clothing, transportation, legal counsel . . ."

"Like when someone wants a divorce?" I interrupted. "You help people get divorced?"

"We do have court advocates and an attorney on our staff to help with divorce filings and protective orders."

"Thank you," I replied. "So, can anyone come to your office at any time?"

"We have donation and office hours here, so visitors would need to make an appointment. Our building is guarded by security to protect our clients and staff," she said.

"But what if someone is being hit," I continued. I still didn't have the language of domestic violence down fully. "Can they come to you? Will you help them when they get there?"

"Yes," she replied. "We'll get her to the right place."

Thanking her, I quickly hung up the phone and erased the call history. I had clothes; I had a bit of money from the grocery stash. I had enough for bus fare, and while she was talking, I'd googled the route to their office from my apartment. I had everything I needed to get out—except the desire.

A part of my story that I've maintained is that I never wanted to leave my husband. And this is the beauty of a human heart. It can be crushed or broken, but it is inconceivably resilient. My heart always bounced back in his direction. And I never lost hope that H. could change. What I lost was the faith that he would change. And the only reason I left, the only reason I got on that bus a few days later, is because I decided that I wanted to live more than I wanted to be married to him.

Later that night, our home was peaceful. He made dinner for us while our new puppy chewed a slipper that I'd long given over to developing puppy teeth. We sat on the couch and watched television—our go-to was *Wheel of Fortune*, a game show he was particularly good at. We cuddled, kissed. I fell asleep. He woke me up so I could get in bed, and after I brushed my teeth and crawled in, he kissed my forehead like he always did, then headed off to the living room to quietly play his keyboard.

I didn't know for sure if I would leave the next morning, or the next. Or the next. The least developed part of my plan was the *when*. I had the *how* and the *where* down. But not the *when*.

A few days later, I woke up to H. kissing my shoulder, heavy arms draped over my side.

"Good morning, Stinky," he said. I laughed and said good morning back. Stinky was a nickname I'd been blessed with about a year earlier when I'd kissed him before I'd brushed my teeth one day.

"You good?"

"Yep, I'm good, boo," I said. And I *was* good.

He got up to take a shower, and I got up to make him some coffee to go. Thirty or so minutes later, he walked to the kitchen and grabbed his messenger bag off of the floor by the counter. I handed him his coffee in his favorite black travel mug, no cream or sugar, and he leaned in for a kiss.

"Love you," he said.

"Love you, too."

I didn't watch him pull away in the car like I always did. I didn't want that to be my last memory of his face, his body. I wanted to remember him kissing me, saying "I love you," smiling at me.

I grabbed a bath towel and walked to the bathroom—the same bathroom where, a few months earlier, I'd made my decision. I looked around at my rainbow-patterned flip flops by the tub, our yellow hand towel freshly washed, on its rack. The bath mat neatly in place.

After my shower, I got dressed and took the pup out. We'd only had him a few weeks, so I hadn't really bonded with him that much, but I knew I'd miss him anyway.

"You be good," I said to the puppy, rubbing his little head. "Look after H. for me."

I locked the small crate and sat on the couch for a second. Then the burning came. It started deep in my throat and wrapped around my head, until my eyes lost the control I'd had over them all morning. Fighting it seemed like an exercise in futility, so I gave myself permission to cry, just for a few minutes, so that the tears would not drown me into inaction.

Walking unhurriedly through the apartment, I touched random things—his keyboard, the kitchen counter, the walls, my nightstand. The closet door handle, the light switch, my shoes, my getaway bag. The thermostat, which I turned to seventy-five, just how he liked it. My keys, which I placed on the counter. The doorknob, then the inside door lock, then the outside doorknob.

I left the keys on purpose; if I locked myself out then I couldn't change my mind. The bus was scheduled to arrive in twenty minutes, and I could make it to the bus stop in fifteen. So, I started walking—slowly at first, but then faster, with a little more intention, in case he returned home for some reason. The quick pace turned into a light jog the more I thought about H. seeing me, and soon I found myself running the last few minutes to the bus stop. Out of breath, I sat down on the bench in the late morning Texas sun. The bus pulled up right on time, and I stepped on quickly, as if this was the most urgent ride of my life.

"Hello!" I remember the bus driver said, clearly excited to see another day.

I smiled and said hi, then sat in the seat directly behind him. I chose not to look back at the apartment complex.

The stop nearest to the domestic violence agency was about a block from their building. I have a great sense of direction; my dad taught me to always memorize the roads that lead to where you're going so you'll know how to get back. My instinct is to create memory photographs of landmarks and street names so I'll recognize where I am, in any city I go to. Since I'd been on this street before, riding with H., it only took a few seconds to figure out which direction to walk when I got off the bus.

What I hadn't planned for however, was a nondescript building with no "Domestic Violence Agency Here!" sign. Panicked, I walked up and down the strip mall plaza, passing a McDonald's and check cashing place.

"How the hell is there no sign?" I asked no one, out loud.

After a few minutes, I walked into the McDonald's.

"Welcome to McDonald's, what can I get you today?" a guy asked.

"Um, hi," I mumbled. "Is there a . . . domestic violence place near here?"

The guy looked me over, equal parts judgy and uneasy.

"Yeah, it's in the shopping center right there, behind the back."

Behind the back. That's why I couldn't find it. *Smart*, I thought. Though terrifying—if you just left your husband, rode a bus here, and can't find it.

I walked back to the strip mall plaza. There was a sidewalk alongside the building, and I followed it to the rear. What was there to fear now? Might as well keep going.

When I got to the back of the building, I saw a police officer or security guard—I couldn't tell which—standing by a door. I remembered that the lady I spoke with the other day said that the building was guarded, so I knew I was in the right place.

"Can I help you ma'am?" he said as I walked closer.

"Yes, um, I'm looking for the domestic violence place."

"Do you have an appointment?"

"No," I said. For the first time, I felt embarrassed. I didn't have an appointment for anything. I wasn't an important person coming to have an important meeting about anything. I was just here because the website said domestic violence services, and that's what I needed. "I'm just here to get help."

"Okay," he said. He walkied someone, presumably upstairs in the building. "What's your name?"

"Beverly Gooden," I said, giving my maiden name.

He opened the building door for me and, using a key, activated the elevator. A few seconds later, the door opened, and he touched the "2" button for me.

"They'll take care of you," he said. I got in the elevator and watched the doors close slowly. The elevator seemed worn, aching from years of bearing the weight of broken hearts, transporting them to their next destination.

And here I was, the next heart it had to haul. Scared but certain. Tired but clear. Tracing more scars along my arms than I used to have, but I was whole. Carrying a heavier body than I used to carry, but I felt beautiful. Less sure of myself, or who I wanted to be, than I was when I left Chicago to be with my boyfriend, but happy, free, and ready. Ready for my new path, praying it would converge with peace, and would belong to only myself.

So—you're *free*. You left the situation; you have renewed vision.

The first thing you want to do is go far, far away. As far as possible. Maybe Canada. Or Antarctica. Believe me, I understand. But here's the thing: If you're married and you move out of state, your divorce case will be significantly prolonged.

First thing's first: If you are in immediate danger and the closest safe place is in another state or country, go there if you can. Throw everything I'm about to write to the wind and run for your life.

The most dangerous time in an abusive relationship is the two weeks after departure. Seventy-six percent of women who have left abusive relationships report instances of post-separation violence (physical violence, rape, verbal threats, stalking, etc.). Find a safe place and *go there*.

In my case, there was no post-separation violence. There were phone calls, texts, and emails—all of which made me miss him and want to go back, but no violence. Although I was afraid, I knew I was not in danger of being hurt.

I briefly stayed at a women's shelter and then moved into a boarding house with several roommates who were complete strangers. But I felt safety in numbers; although they didn't know me and I didn't know them, their presence would bear witness to any post-separation violence that could occur.

All fifty states have residency requirements in order to file for divorce. In my state of Texas, there were not only state requirements, but county requirements as well. Such requirements can range from thirty days to twelve months, depending on the state. You'll also need to look into local requirements. Many people think the state where you married is the state you must divorce. You can divorce in any state if you meet residency. So, if you must relocate out of state for safety, you can file in that state upon meeting the residency requirements.

It's a tricky situation. But my advice is to do what is best regarding your safety while remaining vigilant about your plan. If your plan is to get out and file immediately, you may need to stay in the area. If your plan is simply to get out and let the chips fall where they may, more power to you. Either way, you should be aware of the residency requirement.

The first place you can look for other resources to help you is at your local domestic violence organization. Unfortunately, many of these organizations are limiting their capacity (or closing their doors due to budget constraints and COVID-19). But all domestic violence organizations offer resource and referral information. Do an internet search for "domestic violence organization [insert your city here]." Alternatively, most city halls, human service departments, all police stations, and some religious institutions offer similar resource information for your area.

Law enforcement stations are required by law to have these referrals. Dialing 411, 911 non-emergency, and 211 in many cities will connect you with someone who has domestic violence information.

Along with information for domestic violence organizations, city halls and human service departments can also provide information regarding food stamps and medical assistance. Some cities even offer cash assistance if you've been locked out of your joint bank account or have no money at all.

If you've never considered assistance, please set your pride to the left. Now is the time that you need help. You will likely not need it forever. But this is just the beginning of your journey, and there are long days ahead. Lift some of the burden by getting help.

The second thing you might need is counseling. Most domestic violence organizations offer free counseling to clients; typically, they offer individual counseling and group therapy. I suggest enrolling in both types if they're free to you. *Counseling helped save my life.* The suicidal ideations I developed in the immediate aftermath of leaving were intense, and counseling helped me get through that. Not only did I meet people who were in various stages of their healing journey, I was provided with basic essentials (toothpaste, deodorant, etc.), physical protection (an armed police officer stood watch at the entrance of the building), and a sense of community. Divorce puts your immediate family unit through the shredder. Friends will disappear. Otherwise rational people you've known for years will become judgmental and say ridiculous things. Everyone will suddenly be a relationship expert.

Genuine community cannot be undervalued during this time. A lifeline of people stronger than you, more experienced than you, and who understand what you're going through, is waiting with open arms. Be open to the help—open to making new friends, and open to the possibilities of tomorrow.

Lastly, I want to say that I see you. I know this is a big step. You will cry. I still cry, even a decade later. A gigantic, burning lump will appear in your throat when you're just trying to put your shoes on. This process really, really sucks. But please don't let that stop you from getting the help you need.

Chapter 5

A THEORY OF JUSTICE

"I believe that all organizing is science fiction—that we are shaping the future we long for and have not yet experienced."
—adrienne maree brown

Domestic violence is a social justice issue. In the last chapter I wrote briefly about the intersection of race and intimate partner violence. I want to go further in this chapter and touch on what I think is an important point if we're considering how different survivors survive, and that is the effect that issues of racism and poverty have on access to domestic violence aid. I will also describe four ways that we can create a more just system for all survivors of abuse.

While it's true that intimate partner violence affects all people, the data shows trends indicating that Black women, and more specifically, Black trans women, are at a significantly higher risk of being a victim of this type of crime. The danger in not addressing the cultural factors involved in domestic violence is that society becomes less sensitive to the particular needs of a community and less willing to target that community for outreach, help, and mutual aid.

Natalie Sokoloff, a professor at John Jay College of Criminal Justice, writes, "The traditional feminist approach to domestic violence has generally been to emphasize the common experiences in the interests of forging a strong feminist movement to end abuse. However, this approach has increasingly been questioned by scholars and activists who recognize the need to give voice to women marginalized by the largely white, middle-class feminist movement."[1]

Mikki Kendall, a writer who created the #solidarityisforwhitewomen Twitter hashtag in 2013, writes about the exclusion of women of color from feminist movements in her book *Hood Feminism*. She writes,

> A one-size-fits-all approach to feminism is damaging, because it alienates the very people it is supposed to serve, without ever managing to support them. For women of color, the expectation that we prioritize gender over race, that we treat the patriarchy as something that gives all men the same power, leaves many of us feeling isolated. When the obstacles you face vary by race and class, then so too do your priorities. After all, for women who are struggling to keep themselves housed, fed, and clothed, it's not a question of working hard enough. They are leaning in, but not in search of equal pay or "having it all"; their quest for equal pay starts with equal access to education and opportunity. They need feminism to recognize that everything that affects women is a feminist issue, whether it be food insecurity or access to transit, schools, or a living wage. Does that mean that every feminist has to be at every event, know every detail of every struggle? No. It does, however, mean that the language surrounding whatever issues feminists choose to focus on should reflect an understanding of how the issue's impact varies for women in different socioeconomic positions.[2]

If our approach to feminism must be inclusive and considerate of socioeconomic and identity differences, then so must our approach to aiding victims of domestic violence. It's not enough to note that victims experience this type of violence differently, or that statistically a certain type of victim is more at risk, but we must design our systems of aid in a way that prioritizes the needs of these survivors.

In her research, Beth Richie, professor of gender and women's studies at the University of Illinois at Chicago, found that poor women of color are "most likely to be in both dangerous intimate relationships and dangerous social positions." She argues that "the antiviolence movement's avoidance of race seriously compromises the transgressive and transformative potential of the antiviolence movement's potential [to] radically critique various forms of social domination."[3]

And in terms of social dominance, Black women across the world have less access to resources that could be life-saving due to our historical position within hierarchies. Being at considerable risk of abuse, but also at risk of racism, sexism, poverty, and discrimination, Black women are left vulnerable to sustained domestic violence. And I use Black women in an inclusive way; Black American, African, Afro-Latino, Afro-Caribbean, and so on. Similar issues also persist in other communities of color, such as Indigenous and Latinx women.

Rebecca Miles-Doan, who studies ecological theory, found that rates of violence between intimate partners are higher in low-income neighborhoods in the United States due to resources deprivation.[4] Unemployment, poverty, and economic disadvantage thusly directly contribute to the high rate of domestic violence in economically disadvantaged communities. Furthermore, domestic violence is three times more likely to occur in households where the (cisgender) husband is unemployed or underemployed than those that are employed full time.[5] A study of risk factors also revealed that low-income males with less education and job status are more likely to engage in domestic violence.[6]

Finally, in the essay "Toward a Theory of Race, Crime, and Urban Inequality," Robert Sampson writes about the United States, "It is common knowledge that Black Americans are more likely to live in the socially and economically disadvantaged environments that generate higher crime rates."[7] Why is that? Because those environments have been created for Black Americans, via land and wage theft to residential segregation and housing discrimination. In a 2014 article for *The Atlantic*, renowned writer Ta-Nehisi Coates notes,

> If you sought to advantage one group of Americans and disad-
> vantage another, you could scarcely choose a more graceful
> method than housing discrimination. Housing determines access
> to transportation, green spaces, decent schools, decent food, de-
> cent jobs, and decent services. Housing affects your chances of
> being robbed and shot as well as your chances of being stopped
> and frisked. And housing discrimination is as quiet as it is dead-
> ly. It can be pursued through violence and terrorism, but it
> doesn't need it. Housing discrimination is hard to detect, hard to
> prove, and hard to prosecute. Even today most people believe
> that Chicago is the work of organic sorting, as opposed to segre-
> gationist social engineering. Housing segregation is the weapon
> that mortally injures, but does not bruise. [8]

It is no surprise that Black Americans are hesitant to seek assistance from systems that not only trivialize their claims of abuse, but also created the environments where they are disadvantaged in the first place. But it does not have to be this way, and there is still time to correct the past and equitize the future. *Poverty does not have to exist. It persists by design.* In Coates's housing example above, the segregation itself is a design. Communities of color are pushed and segregated further away from established needs, like medical offices and grocery stores. And then, grocers fail to open new stores in poor communities even though everyone has to eat. All that's left then, are small convenience stores with more Cheetos than apples, creat-ing a position ripe for long-term health challenges due to poor nutri-tion, none of which is the fault of the community who was forced to that area of town. *Poverty is by design.* Come on now, we have billionaires fighting to ride in a spaceship to a potential luxury space resort. If each billionaire chose just one social issue to solve, soci-oeconomic outcomes would look different in just a decade. *Poverty does not have to exist.*

So, what can we do? Not only for Black people, but for every victim of abuse? I'm convinced that we can do so much more in the area of domestic violence, but we need the support of government, communities, philanthropists, spaceship billionaires, and, most importantly, the people. So many of us, regardless of gender identity, but particularly those who identify as women, suffer at the hands of abusive partners simply because we are afraid that we won't be able to survive, economically, without them, as the systems that *should* help us survive are hard to access. With limited employment history, little financial stability, and discrimination, survivors are finding it difficult to survive.

My vision is fourfold: Love, Protect, Educate, and Reform.

LOVE

"Love" is not a word you typically hear after being presented with an argument for systematic change, but understand that love encourages *responsiveness and care*, love is by nature transformative. adrienne maree brown is a writer, doula, and activist who writes often about feminism, transformative justice, and, in this case, love. In her book *Emergent Strategy: Shaping Change, Changing Worlds* she writes sharply about the metamorphic power of love:

> One thing I have observed: When we are engaged in acts of love, we humans are at our best and most resilient. The love in romance that makes us want to be better people, the love of children that makes us change our whole lives to meet their needs, the love of family that makes us drop everything to take care of them, the love of community that makes us work tirelessly with broken hearts. Perhaps humans' core function is love. Love leads us to observe in a much deeper way than any other emotion. If love were the central practice of a new generation of organizers and spiritual leaders, it would have a massive impact on what was considered organizing. If the goal was to increase the love, rather than winning or dominating a constant opponent, I think we could actually imagine liberation from constant oppression.

We would suddenly be seeing everything we do, everyone we meet, not through the tactical eyes of war, but through eyes of love. We would see that there's no such thing as a blank canvas, an empty land or a new idea—but everywhere there is complex, ancient, fertile ground full of potential. We would organize with the perspective that there is wisdom and experience and amazing story in the communities we love, and instead of starting up new ideas/organizations all the time, we would want to listen, support, support, collaborate, merge, and grow through fusion, not competition. We would understand that the strength of our movement is in the strength of our relationships, which could only be measured by their depth.[9]

Love is not the key to social change, desire is. We've got to *want* to change things. But love is the cornerstone of change. A cornerstone is the first stone laid during the construction of a building's foundation; all other stones are set in relation to this stone's position. The cornerstone determines the outcome of the whole structure. If we focus more on caring for others out of genuine compassion than working to secure our own place within the social hierarchy, not only would we be more successful in change, but we'd lay the foundation for a better system, a new structure for future victims of violence.

PROTECT

Keystone and critical to the interruption of domestic violence is protection. Any survivor of a crime can attest that the first thing we seek is safety. We're traumatized. We do not know what to do. Sometimes we have nowhere to go. All we know is that we need to be protected from the person who hurt us. This, in my opinion, is a fair request and a human rights issue. It's not only fair to ask this of society, but survivors should expect that the help they need will be provided generously.

Our government, legal system, and our communities should seek to protect a victim of domestic violence at any cost. It is our calling

as members of humanity to ensure the protection of the most vulnerable among us. And I live by that. I'm not talking about the limited
methods of protection that always lead to carceral punishment, because punishment does not automatically protect and protection is
not *only* the removal from a harmful situation. Protection is the
continued promise that the community, system, and law will come
through to meet a survivor's needs, however long that need is
present.

Part of those needs are access to resources and *equitable treatment*. In *When Love Is Not Enough*, Dr. Mary Elsbernd, my graduate school program director writes,

> Access to resources necessary for humane and authentic human
> living includes attention to equity and justice. For instance, when
> children play and eat together, issues tend to be resolved by
> absolute equality in the piece of candy or in the time allotted to a
> favorite toy. Equality in access to resources, however, does not
> typically end up in justice. Not sameness, but fairness or equity
> often provides a more fitting standard of justice. Equitable treat-
> ment demands personal action which does not discriminate on
> the basis of relationships (e.g., life status, station, association),
> embodiment (e.g., gender, race, ethnicity), social location (e.g.,
> class, language, national origin), or accountable agency (e.g.,
> religion). Justice as equitable treatment recognizes that differ-
> ences require fair treatment. [10]

Protection is also vital for those advocates and activists who have
made the issue of domestic violence their day-to-day, professional
work. Many advocates deal with issues like burnout, stress, lack of
managerial support, and low pay. How can this be if we're going to
create a safe, healthy environment for survivors, providing adequate
services to those who seek help? Every year it seems like I read
news articles of a shelter closing, an organization losing funding, or
federal funding being reallocated. Where will survivors go if there
are few advocates left to help?

Tanya Grant's 2014 research study, "Domestic Violence Victims—An Examination of Advocates' Experiences and Impact on

Services,"[11] spoke with domestic violence victim advocates and found that many advocates are suffering from burnout. They do not feel valued by their organization in terms of training and pay, and they don't feel connected to domestic violence professionals in other organizations inside and outside of their communities. After identifying seven common themes among the research subjects, including lack of management support and unrealistic expectations from both clients and organizational leaders, Dr. Grant concluded,

> This study is significant due to its exploration of the lived experiences of domestic violence victim advocates who have worked in the field for various periods of time. Whether advocates were newly employed (six months) or tenured (ten plus years), the feelings they expressed were mutual. In addition, the advocates interviewed were employed by various agencies, thus indicating that this is a problem across agencies. However, the irony is that ninety percent of the advocates interviewed expressed that their personal interest or passion is the reason why they continue doing the work, regardless of the organizational flaws. Therefore, it stands to reason that agencies should be embracing the employees who truly love what they do and providing them with a great environment in which to do such work; only management can do these things.

Advocates *want to do the work*. They are there, working in this field, not completely out of necessity but because they have a passion for it. To both nurture and protect that passion, organizational leaders must take responsibility for ensuring advocates and staff are supported, heard, and trained.

EDUCATE

We live in a generation that thrives on social media. In 2010, Twitter and Facebook users helped fuel the flames of revolution in Egypt. This international awareness helped overthrow the Egyptian government and initiate the process of reformation. In 2014, the hashtag #BringBackOurGirls trended, demanding a return of the 276 Nigerian school girls taken by Boko Haram. In 2017 we had, of course, the #MeToo movement, when survivors of sexual assault spoke out en masse. And in 2020, we watched the entire world respond on social media to the murder of George Floyd at the hands of a police officer in Minneapolis. International movements and hundreds of millions of dollars flowed to popular organizations because of the attention.

With exposure tools such as this, it is our duty to educate people about the stories of abuse survivors who may not fit a Perfect Victim ideation. Survivors who have been incarcerated after defending themselves from abuse. Immigrants who have been deported after reporting abuse. Trans women who are targeted and murdered by intimate partners. Or Indigenous women who have been missing for years.

Social media has changed the way we interact with one another and the speed at which information is shared. News of the attack on the U.S. Capitol by white supremacists and self-proclaimed patriots in January 2021 broke on Twitter and spread throughout the nation in seconds. Organizations such as the National Domestic Violence Hotline and Times Up have a large presence on social media. And it is not for lack of public awareness that domestic violence public service announcements (PSAs) and news does not seem to spread. These organizations post daily and are met with limited engagement.

My thought is that we need to make intimate partner violence education a standard part of American education, beginning in elementary school. This is the age that children are first told that other kids, usually little boys, hit girls "because they like you." The assertion being that pain equals interest or love and the infliction of pain is a tender initiation. We have to intercept those messages and replace them with blatant discussions about healthy interactions. That education should be well funded and considered as important as math and science, coupled with social media campaigns that reiterate information about abuse on a constant loop. There can be no lull in intensity; our efforts must be as urgent as the COVID-19 pandemic information cycle. Social media is a tool, and it's how we use it, when, how often, and the content we share that makes all the difference.

REFORM

Finally, I believe in policy change. While it is necessary to rally around the victim with help from the community and justice system, the main source of help should be from lawmakers. Victims' advocates have been working for years to ensure the issue of domestic violence is kept at the forefront of reform. We've come a long way in terms of recognizing the crime of domestic violence, but we've got a long way to go. Until long-term funding is dedicated to aiding victims, and until laws are in place that ensure the continued safety of victims, we have work to do.

A primary concern of all abuse survivors is safety. And it should be the focus of all institutions (faith-based institutions included) that the victim who comes to them for help is kept safe. The problem with faith-based institutions is that they have been too concerned about the *state of the marriage* rather than the *safety of the victim.* This practice must end. Whether the marriage survives is irrelevant and a nonfactor. What is important is that the victim is away from danger.

The most overlooked area is the mental health of the survivor. In the 2015 book *The Body Keeps the Score* psychiatrist Bessel van der Kolk, who has faced his own employee mistreatment controversy in recent years,[12] writes, "Traumatized people chronically feel unsafe inside their bodies: The past is alive in the form of gnawing interior discomfort. Their bodies are constantly bombarded by visceral warning signs, and, in an attempt to control these processes, they often become expert at ignoring their gut feelings and in numbing awareness of what is played out inside. They learn to hide from their selves."[13]

It is difficult to function in society without help to deal with the traumatic stress that has rewired the very chemical makeup of your brain. Without mental health treatment, survivors could very easily slip through the cracks. Being safe and legally safeguarded is not enough; the quality of our mental state is critically important to moving from an abusive situation to becoming fully functional and thriving within modern society.

Part II

Chapter 6

REINVENTION

"I'll just take my name."
—Tina Turner

There's a great scene in the 1971 film *Willy Wonka and the Chocolate Factory*. Willy Wonka, a witty, charismatic, but kind of spooky candy-factory owner, has selected five kids, via a golden ticket lottery, to tour his factory one afternoon. After introducing himself and setting some ground rules, Willy Wonka leads the kids and their chosen family member to a brightly colored, massive playground where everything, including the chocolate river flowing through the scene, is made of candy. Like, everything.

"Hold your breath, make a wish, count to three . . ." Wonka says, as he dances down the grand stairs.

I sat at White Rock Lake Park in Dallas and looked out over the lake that was, sadly, not made of chocolate. But I held my breath, made several wishes, and counted to three. It was so beautiful to be there for as long as I wanted. It was one of the first places I went after moving into the boarding house. I wanted to see things, meet new people, and experience life like I was a kid. The world was my Chocolate Factory, and I wanted to taste every leaf, rock, and fountain.

Which sounds corny, but it's true. I wanted to taste life. I wanted to see all the things that I hadn't seen. I was in Texas, but not of my own accord or my own will, but because that's where he wanted to go. So now I wanted to see Texas for myself. I wanted to see life for myself.

I survived. I was here. I was free. But who was I now? Because I was no longer the person I was before I got married. I think it's fair to say that that person is gone forever. I did not mourn her in the way that most grief requires. I celebrated her; honored her, who carried me through childhood, high school, and college. That me was a cool person, somewhat naïve but learning, loving, and growing. That person's opinions? Their goals? Their likes and dislikes? I don't even remember them now. So then, who was I? And if you are new to surviving, *who are you*?

I've been thinking a lot about identity: how we use it, what we call ourselves and when, how those things change over time. Why they matter, why they don't always. Which identities are static—for example, I'm Black and will always be—and which can often be inconstant—for example, ability. Acknowledging that the choreography of identity is important because of our intersections but also deeply uncertain because of fluidity.

While I was living in Chicago attending grad school in 2008, I did not have health insurance. I couldn't afford it. So I found a low-income women's clinic that offered a sliding scale for basic services, like pelvic exams and "well woman" visits. I'd been in pain for a few weeks, a deep, sharp, heavy pain, mostly in my lower abdominal region but sometimes in my back. At first, I thought it might be an advanced form of cramping since my periods had become super heavy a few months before. I couldn't make it an hour without having to change my pad or tampon; my flow was so constant that I wore dark pants every day of my period.

So I made an appointment at this women's clinic—a referral from my grad school's student health office. I arrived early to my appointment and checked in, making sure to circle the "sliding scale" option under Patient Self Pay. Then I sat down in the waiting room alongside four other patients, waiting for my turn.

A few minutes after my appointment time, a nurse with curly brown hair wearing pink scrubs opened the door and stepped partially into the waiting room.

"Beverly?" she asked, scanning the room for a response.

"That's me," I said, hopping up out of my chair to walk over to her.

"Hi honey, come on back."

If you've never had a pap smear, count your blessings. It is never pleasant, always awkward, and sometimes very uncomfortable. After explaining my symptoms to the doctor who had walked in to introduce herself, I got undressed and positioned myself on the table, feet in stirrups, bustle of the city streets outside the window.

"I think I know why you might be having issues with your cycle," said the doctor, after completing a pelvic examination. "Have you heard of fibroids?"

"No," I said.

"Fibroids are tumors that can grow inside or outside of the uterus," she said. "I know I poked around a bit, but it feels like you may have a large one."

Again, I'd never heard of fibroids so I assumed it was something a pill could take care of, you know, to shrink them or something.

A few weeks and $150 later, an ultrasound confirmed the presence of not one, but three fibroids. My options were to start birth control pills in hopes of easing the symptoms of the fibroids, or to schedule a surgery to remove them. I chose birth control since I couldn't imagine being able to afford surgery. I could barely afford the ultrasound.

And so it was that way for the next eleven years. I was on and off birth control, switching between brands or stopping them altogether, until I noticed that my periods were heavier than ever before. One of the brands I tried made me stop having periods for the three years I took the pills. But once I took a break from them, all the symptoms of fibroids returned, only this time, much worse. Not only did I have heavy periods, the period would not *stop*; I frequently had nineteen-to twenty-five-day periods and would bleed the entire time. Aside from the bleeding, I could not seem to get enough rest due to pelvic pain that interrupted my sleep. Something was putting pressure on my bladder, and I could not make it through the night without getting up four to five times, sometimes more. Sex was so painful that I just stopped having it.

By that time, I had a full-time job, which in the United States is normally tied to employer-sponsored health insurance. I usually saw my gynecologist for the annual pap smear visit or any intermittent issues, like yeast infections. But after my third month of nonstop bleeding, I made an emergency appointment.

Twelve. That's the number of fibroids that had grown over the last eleven years, my birth control pills masking the symptoms of the tumors. While the initial three were outside of my uterus, now there were several growing on the *inside* of my uterus. And one tumor on the outside of my uterus had reached ten centimeters in diameter.

So now, my options were to remove the largest fibroids and hope the others would not grow, or remove the entire uterus.

My biological mother gave birth to me when she was just a teenager, which I consider an act of bravery. After her labor, she left me in the care of the hospital—another act of bravery—knowing that she couldn't raise me herself. I was adopted by the Gooden family when I was very young, too young to remember the details of foster care. I write all of that to say, I have always embraced alternative paths to mothering, knowing that giving birth is not a prerequisite for it. I've also always been on the fence about mothering at all. Toward the end of my uterus-having days, I decided that I did not want to give birth; that any child in my life would not come from my body, and that being childless was a reasonable, valid path as well.

So, this was an easy decision for me, not traumatic or heartbreaking. I chose total hysterectomy; removing my uterus, cervix, fallopian tubes, and, of course, the twelve fibroids, all benign. I left my ovaries inside, so I would be able to extract eggs and freeze them as a way to keep several options open. But having my uterus removed meant I would no longer be a birthing person, which had been part of my identity whether I embraced birthing or not.

When I had a hysterectomy, I could no longer identify as some-one who had a uterus. I began asking myself questions like what, before this very moment, was my reason for identifying as a wom-an? Was that identity connected to reproduction? If so, what is my identity now that pregnancy is impossible? If not, why should any-thing change in how I identify? Do I still consider myself a woman? If so, what exactly *carries* that identity for me? What if I considered not identifying as a woman at all anymore? What are the implica-tions of rejecting a gender identity altogether?

And why hadn't I thought through this at all before?

A huge part of my reinvention was deciding who I am now and what I identify as. And there were some identities that I tilted heavi-ly toward and others that I rejected.

In the months after leaving my marriage, I did not consider my-self a survivor. Nothing in my material life, save for my physical presence, survived. Yes, I was alive, but what else did I have? Nothing. So I clung to "victim" as a descriptor and held on to that for years.

Identifying as a victim gave me peace in a way because the descriptor indicates a crime had been committed. And I wanted that to be clear: My husband had done something to me that was unac-ceptable by legal standards. That gave me a sense of justice, even without directly involving the carceral state. It made me feel seen in a way that "survivor" did not.

But I survived; I am a survivor. Surviving and survival are both pieces of my identity. So I go by both terms now, as I know the value of being in community with those who embrace the term "victim" and those who do not. And I make it a point to call people exactly what they identify as, if it's been made clear by them. In the context of abuse, if someone identifies as a survivor, I'll call them that. If they identify as a victim, I call them that. If neither fits, I don't assign any identity to them at all.

Then there was the court-mandated identity change—married to single. And I had absolutely no idea who I was as a single person again. But since I couldn't identify as a married person or a partner, by choice, I needed to figure that out. What does single me like?

Does single me stretch out in the bed at night or does she sleep on one side? Who does single me want to talk to?

And so, while it may seem small, choosing and understanding how you identify now that abuse is no longer a part of your life, while remaining a part of your *story*, can be useful.

∽

I knew Tina Turner would be prominent in my life the moment I heard her sing a song in which romantic love was decentered. Not that love shouldn't be centered at times, it's just that, in the midst of a sea of sappy love songs and a past divorce, Tina metaphorically said, "Not so fast!" which I thought was pretty bold.

I feel a deep connection to Tina Turner. Our birthdays are two days apart. We both escaped abuse while in Dallas, Texas. We're both musicians. We both believe in psychic gifts. Ms. Turner is incredible for many, many reasons. But right now, I want to focus on how she chose to reclaim, or rather, maintain and reinvent, her identity after she left an abusive husband.

In part II of *Tina*, the HBO documentary released in March 2021, Tina Turner describes what happened in her divorce hearing.

"I got nothing; no money, no house, no car," she explains. "The judge called us into the chamber and I said, 'Actually, there is something he has that I want.' That's when I realized that I could use Tina to become a business. And so, I said, 'I'll just take my name.' Ike fought a little bit because he knew what I would do with it. And it was through court that I got it, Tina."

Tina Turner reclaimed the name given to her by her ex-husband, refined it, and reinvented herself using it. It's both brilliant and inspirational.

Now you might think Tina Turner is a global phenomenon, and her survival story is completely unrelated to yours and mine. And that is partially true, in terms of access and connections. But when Tina left, she was penniless. She had nothing but her life.

The night that she left, she maneuvered across a highway, cross-ing incoming traffic, and nearly escaping a truck collision. When she got to the Dallas Ramada Inn, she said to the hotel manager, "I have had a fight with my husband. Will you give me a room?" Tina only had a Mobil credit card and thirty-six cents. She promised the hotel manager that if he gave her a room that evening, she would repay him in full one day.

> "I believe that if you'll just stand up and go, life will open up for you." —Tina Turner

About domestic violence, Tina writes in her memoir, *My Love Story*: "For anyone who's in an abusive relationship, I say this: nothing can be worse than where you are now. Nothing. If you get up and leave, if you rise from the ashes, life will open up for you again."

What if your reinvention led you to a life of good fortune? What if, after your leaving, you found that life opened up for you in boundless ways?

Along the way, especially when I had thoughts of returning to H., I constantly asked myself, "Who can I be now that I'm free to be?"

There is no standard way of how to be in the world. You are who you are, and whoever you are is okay. The goal is to move through the world in a way that brings comfort, peace, and stability while actively reducing your harm footprint. I'm going to talk more about harm reduction in another chapter, but it's important to know that your existence is not harmful, regardless of what your former partner may say. Your decision to move on from a relationship is not causing harm. It may cause sadness to your former partner, but *you have this right*. The right to move on, the right to rebuild, the right to live how you want.

I was excited to start my new life, though I desperately missed H. There were times I would wake up in the middle of the night in the boarding house, covered in sweat, confused about where I was at that moment. I wanted to go home, but not enough to give up this new life I was creating. And that life looked terrible at first. A boarding house is a loud, uncomfortable place to be.

The boarding house was a six-bedroom, three-and-a-half-bathroom brown brick McMansion in a north suburb of Dallas. While the exterior was beautiful, the inside looked and felt cold; there were no home decorations or furnishings outside of the master suite. The owner made it clear that visitors were not allowed and refused to put a sofa or dining set in the common areas in an effort to enforce that rule. The heat was turned down low in the winter, no higher than maybe seventy degrees, and the air conditioning stayed off in the spring unless Texas temperatures went above ninety degrees. "Close the shades and it'll stay cool in your room," the owner of the house would say.

I was the final resident to move in; aside from the owner who lived in the master suite, there were four college students renting rooms in the house. There was just one refrigerator located in the garage for all of us to share, and we were not allowed to use the kitchen to cook; any cooking had to be done outside of the boarding house. I didn't have friends or family in the area whose kitchen I could use to cook in, so I bought an electric kettle from Walmart and had ramen noodles for dinner most nights. My standard breakfast was a Styrofoam cup of instant oatmeal and brewed coffee I made in my black plastic one-cup coffee maker that heated the bottled water *way* too hot and frequently burned my fingers.

Although I felt relatively safe in the house, I had no community there, and community is the path to freedom. I grew up slathered in the love of various communities. My big, loving extended family, the church community, music community, organizing community, art community. But in that boarding house I only had myself. It felt lonely in a way that I hope never to experience again. I landed in Texas because my husband wanted to be there, and now, I had to find my way out. And I would eventually, but at that moment, I had to find my way period.

As I mentioned before, I'd stopped working while I was married. Even then I knew that a gap in my resume would cause issues when looking for a job. And I'm not gonna front; I padded my resume. I stretched the dates of a job or two to make up for gaps, added a few technical skills I definitely didn't have. I decided I could get a clerical role based on the fact that my first job out of undergrad was as an administrative assistant. I applied to at least twenty jobs a day for two weeks and got no response.

So then, strategy number two: look for nonprofit jobs. I thought, I've just experienced domestic violence, and I have a few years of nonprofit experience. Surely a domestic violence organization will hire me to do *something*. No, that did not happen. And truly, I applied to fifteen or so domestic violence organizations in and out of state, explicitly stating that not only was I a survivor but I also had professional experience in nonprofit administration, and I never got a call back.

Next, I turned to temp agencies, and this is what brought me relief from the job search. I finally got a call back from a temp agency recruiter about an office job.

"What kind of office job?" I asked, wanting to make sure it was something I could do, since I'd padded my resume with fiction.

"Data entry," the recruiter said. "You can type, right?"

I could type. In fact, I'd been typing since I was a little kid. Thanks, Mavis Beacon.

"Yes."

"Can you take a typing test?"

"Yes, that's no problem."

It was kind of a problem. I didn't have a car and ridesharing did not exist yet.

"Is it something I can take at a library?"

"No, you have to come in to take it here."

So yes, a problem.

"I don't have a car right now, and I don't know if I can get a ride from someone."

The recruiter hesitated.

"If you don't have a car to get here then how would you get to a job?" she asked.

I felt like the walls of the phone were caving in on me. I hadn't been sleeping well and had only really been eating ramen and bread.

I hadn't thought through the transportation issue in full because I was hungry and depressed.

I didn't answer the recruiter's question because I knew I'd figure it out. I had to. Instead, I asked when the next available appointment for the typing test was. We scheduled the test two days out, which gave me two days to find a way to get there.

"Hey," I said.

"Hey."

"I think I have a job offer and . . . I mean, I don't have a car right now. I need some help, some money."

H. paused for a few seconds.

"Okay."

We hadn't been speaking. In fact, save for a few conversations, texts mostly, I hadn't heard from H. since I left. But he was the only person I knew in town who could get enough money to me, and quickly.

"I really appreciate it."

"Yeah," he continued. "I'll put half of my check into the account today. Let me know if you need more."

This moment is what complicates my feelings about H. and demonstrates how complicated these relationships truly are. I will never defend H. for his violence. And I'll always have the memory of that violence. But in this moment, he could have chosen to treat that money as a carrot stick. He could have asked for something in return or used the clear power dynamic as a manipulation tool to say, "You wouldn't need this money if you came home." But instead, in this moment, he helped me pursue a new life. A life he knew he'd never be involved in. A life without him. In this moment he chose to help right a wrong that he'd been responsible for, and I believe he made that choice consciously.

And I'm so thankful to him for that.

Something I've been working through as I write: I think it's okay to mourn complicated people so long as we don't let our feelings of sadness absolve them of the pain that they've caused us and others. I think we can hold space for both grief and accountability. Grief, because that is a normal part of loss. Accountability, because the loss occurred for a specific reason, one that could have been avoided. And I've discovered that the area between the two, heart-ache and responsibility, makes for a more realistic place to exist while beginning the healing journey. Because both are a resolute; neither grief nor accountability is dependent on the other. They can exist independently, in different emotional spaces, while both being reasonable and true. I mourn the loss of my marriage to H. because I *wanted* that relationship to last, and that is okay. I acknowledge that he was abusive and is accountable for the behavior that resulted in my grief, and that is also okay. Both/and.

The next day, with $500 in hand, I searched through the used car listings on Craigslist hoping to find an old, but drivable, car. I didn't care how old it was, or how it looked. It just needed it to drive.

I found a listing for a 1989 Chevrolet Cavalier. The listing made it clear that this was a "last resort" car with no air conditioning, no sound system, manual windows, and a cracked windshield.

But it ran fine.

I convinced the owner of the car to drive it to the boarding house, with my promise that I would purchase it from him no matter what. He asked for $500; I offered $400. He said $475 was as low as he could go; I told him I only had $450, which was true. The $50 was my grocery money for the week. He looked me over, up and down, trying to locate rust in my armor that would prove I was bluffing. I guess he found no such rust.

"Sold," he said.

I had a car. And after passing my typing test, I had a temp job. I had a room in a boarding house with my own bathroom. Soon I'd have money for regular groceries and gas.

I finally had something, which was more than the nothing I started out with. I had myself, I had hope, and I had a plan. And this, I found, was exactly what I needed.

So, I want to tell you some things that I did during this time, in hopes that they might help you or someone you know in the reinvention process. You're rebuilding while reimagining everything your life could be, now that you can decide those things for yourself.

TAKE CARE OF YOURSELF

Throughout my life I've seen my physical body react to stress in a few specific ways. While I was married, my hair was falling out in droves. But almost as soon as I left my husband, my hair stopped falling out. It never fully returned, but at least my condition changed as the stress eased. I also tend to gain significant weight when I'm stressed, as eating has been a coping mechanism in the past. I'd been taking birth control pills to ensure I did not get pregnant by my husband, and a doctor told me that could be contributing to the weight gain. I didn't mind the weight as far as appearance goes, but it began to have a negative impact on my breathing. So, I set out to lose enough weight so that my breathing normalized.

And the weight did drop off, partly because I stopped the birth control pills, but also because of my limited access to food. While the change was welcomed, the method was not. Regardless, it's important to decide what changes, immediate and long term, you'd like to make and plan for that. Don't stress out if the changes you're planning for take time, particularly if they are physical (they don't have to be).

Abuse takes a toll on your physical body. The violence, the tension, and the stress. Everything. Relatedly, I slept a *lot*. When I wasn't at work, I was sleeping or trying to fall asleep. I'd take thirty-minute naps during my lunch break. If traffic seemed like it would be busy after work, I'd sit in the car and sleep for an hour. I couldn't get enough of sleep now that I could do it whenever I wanted, with no responsibilities other than taking care of my own needs. I needed a lot of rest, and I got it. Even now, I get lots of rest, and I had to come to terms with the importance of rest in my new life. Whenever I lie around for a morning, I always have to tell myself that I'm not "doing nothing," because rest *is* something. But also, doing nothing is *okay*.

Most importantly, I became okay with all parts of me. I began to really like how I look, walk, speak, and smile. I was okay with my alopecia, a scalp condition that causes hair loss, and decided if someone wanted to love me, they had to love that part of me as well. I have belly fat that will not go away with crunches (please stop telling women to do crunches, for the love of God), and I've decided to love it. I named my belly fat "Bella," because that belly fat looks like it's always going to be with me. So, I'll love Bella. I regularly tell myself, "You're okay," or, "You're just fine," because I need to hear it out loud sometimes.

One thing I learned about myself during this time is that I have a lot of untapped strength. I've always had determination and the will to begin again, but my resilience was fortified. And that is good because I had to pull on it to keep going, especially when I had no food. The boarding house only provided a room and bathroom; it was a safe place to sleep and nothing more. My parents did their best to send money—twenty dollars here and there—to help me eat. Any food I had, I bought. And if I could not afford much food, I didn't eat. Trying to do well at work every day is hard when you are hungry, but attempting to rebuild a new life is nearly impossible without secure employment or housing. So, I had the basics but no extras. Being kind to myself, gentle with myself, was especially important during that time.

Housing security, food security, living wages—these things are the foundation of a stable life. Not even a *thriving* life, just a stable one. My husband had two jobs with regular paychecks. I wasn't hungry with him. We weren't middle class, but I didn't have to worry about being unhoused when I was with him. It would have been so easy to go back and be taken care of. But I fought for my freedom. It was hard won. And I learned that I could do anything with enough focus and time.

FIND A (FUN) HOBBY

My husband embraced my hobbies, but only if they involved him. So it was easier just to give them up than try to include him every time I wanted to go somewhere or do something. If I wanted to go for a run, he'd be there too. If I wanted to write, he wanted to read it. But now, I engage in my hobbies without concern for someone else's opinion. And it is *freeing*.

Dating was a nonstarter, but rediscovering my hobbies—and adopting new ones—was top of the list in terms of reinventing my life. For example, I often stayed indoors all day, so about a month after I'd settled into the boarding house, I bought some used roller skates. And man, would I roller skate! In the morning, after work, and sometimes even during my lunch break. Roller skating makes me feel fast and free.

Finding hobbies not only took my mind off of what was going on—separation, job anxiety, undesirable living situation—but it also made me feel alive. I did a lot of reading, catching up with old friends, starting new friendships, and just being. That was one of my new hobbies for sure, just being. Just existing in a place, taking up room. Going to the mall and people-watching. Sitting in a coffee shop. Reading by the lake, of course. Just *present* and *alive*.

EVALUATE YOUR FINANCES

I was so damn broke after I left my husband. I've already told the story of asking for money to buy a car and living on ramen. But I want to emphasize that I had no regular help. Any money I had I made on my own. There were days I wouldn't eat because I had no food. The process for getting approved for food stamps was hell; anyone who tells you that "government assistance" is easy is a liar. It was hellish.

I was on food stamps for a year and when the $92 per month I received didn't cover my food expenses, I would go to food banks for help. Once, I took a two-hour bus ride to a food bank and only walked away with a bag of nearly stale bagels and two cans of soup. I would ration my food out for the week. That life is ugly; it is traumatic in itself.

And it's important to call that out; while abuse happens regardless of socioeconomic status, class implications do play a role in recovery. Once a victim leaves an abusive relationship, their financial position will determine *how* they are able to recover and *when*. The how is in regard to what tools are at their disposal, for example, access to savings, a vehicle, the ability to buy food or quickly rent an apartment. The when is regarding the same things, only how *soon* those resources can be accessed or obtained. My economic recovery depended on bus schedules, the availability of food donations, some mathematical formula that spit out an exact food stamp benefit amount I was eligible for. But for those that have transportation, family with money to give, and food, recovery will happen sooner and with a bit more ease.

The divorce itself did not leave me in debt. But starting my life after I divorced was difficult financially. The part-time temp job I worked paid $12 per hour, and my monthly rent for the boarding house was $600. That left roughly $200 per month for literally everything else I needed.

The reason it's important to evaluate your finances is because, while you may not be able to change your financial circumstance quickly, at least you'll know where to begin and how much you will need. Aside from food, there are other things to consider: fuel for a car, insurance, student loan payments, any credit card or personal loan debt you have, personal care, and more.

But also, your hobbies! I'm not someone who believes that if you're struggling then you've no right to spend any money on fun. Our hobbies keep us alive and engaged. We can't just work all the time; we need to enjoy life. Have fun! Build it into your financial needs. But most of all, know what you need and plan for how to get it. Even if that plan includes asking for help in the form of "no repayment" money. Not borrowed, but given, like a grant. That leads us to the next section.

FIND A SUPPORT SYSTEM

When I left my husband, I didn't tell anyone except my family and close friends. Everyone else eventually found out through word of mouth. I preferred that because it meant fewer questions for me.

One of the first people I told about the abuse was my brother's wife's mother, I call her "Momma T." She had experienced abuse in her past and was able to support me, emotionally, through my transition. She called every few days to ask how I was feeling, if I felt safe. And I knew I could tell her anything, without judgment.

My sister-in-law was also a source of support, but in a different way.

"What do you want to do?" she asked, after I told her I'd moved out of the apartment.

"I don't know."

"Well, whatever you want to do, we support you. If you want to get divorced, we got your back. If you want to go home, we'll still be here for you. But whatever you decide, we love you and got you."

I carry her words with me even now. Some loved ones, when faced with the news that there is abuse in the life of someone they love, immediately demand action. With genuine intentions, they bulldoze into the situation and make a decision for the survivor. *Leave now. You would be stupid to stay. You know better!* Survivors have told me so many variations of those statements.

But the statement "you decide" gave me my power back. And that's what support systems do: they empower you to make your own choices. To make choices for us, when we did not ask you to, is to disempower us and remove our autonomy, making you another person who wants to control our lives. And that is not what is needed.

I know that's hard to hear and might be even harder in action. But remember this: People in your life who want to help you out of a domestic violence situation are there to be a support, not an owner. In all of their love, fear, and concern, it is their job to help, not rule.

I owe my sanity to my sister-in-law. She made me feel like I was back in control of my life, that I would not be letting her down if I decided to go back to him, and that I would not be alone if I decided never to go back to him.

My parents and brother were also a support. A few years after leaving, I learned that my father and brother both had a hard time dealing with the abuse. My father felt sad; he dealt with feelings of failure as a protector, and he felt fooled for trusting H. to care for me. My brother does not like to talk about H. at all, so I do not know the details of his personal pain. But ultimately, they were both able to see past their anger and focus on loving me back to health.

My support system worked to relieve two things: loneliness and instability. I felt unstable for a very long time. My husband had been the steady fixture in my life; my entire existence was anchored in him. So after I left, I felt like I needed to stabilize. Having people around who were supportive and encouraging helped me stay steady. All out of secrets, I was able to have conversations with them about money, depression, suicidal ideation, my wins and joys, and everything in between. Those conversations made me feel safe, and the firm presence of those in my support system created stability when that was the main thing I needed for my life to begin to rebuild.

Reinvention is one of the more exciting parts of surviving abuse. Deciding who you want to be, again, is a gift; not everyone gets a second or third chance to create the life they want to live in. Consider reinvention your greatest asset during the recovery period after abuse. You can choose every new thing that forms the structure of your life.

Chapter 7

TOUCH

"An animal that has survived the terror of a forest fire recognizes the acrid smell of smoke faster than one who has not. A [person] who has survived an abusive relationship becomes hyper-vigilant, determined to protect themself from further danger."
—Elaine Weiss, EdD

The thing about trauma is that it shows up in unexpected ways at unexpected times.

I do not like to be touched by men, and sometimes, not at all. That is hard for me to say because I'm a very affectionate person; I'm a hugger to the point of *squeezing*. I melt into physical contact, and I always have.

I come from a family of people who, molded by the Black Church, knew that hugging, touching, just the act of placing your skin on another person's skin, was an acknowledgment—a way to say, "I see you; you're here, you're alive, and I'm happy about it." But ever since the end of my marriage, I have not enjoyed the touch of men. I tense up when it happens, and 75 percent of the time these are men that I *want* to touch me. These are men who I'm about to have sex with, or men who I've agreed to go out with, and we're leaning in for a hug. Or men who are my friends that I haven't seen in a long time who I know love me without manipulation or violence. And I still don't always like it.

To survive physical abuse is to have your relationship with touch altered. What touch will be good and what touch won't be? You never really know from moment to moment. It could feel gentle, like fingertips slowly tracing your arm in the morning sun. Or it could feel like a sudden, hard impact; a car crash, over and over again within a span of ten minutes.

When you survive abuse, the delineation between positive and negative touch doesn't truly exist, because in abusive situations that line is crossed on such a regular basis that the impact of touch is unpredictable. You hope for a positive touch, but eventually you learn not even to do that. Because that hope for good touch becomes distressing when the reality is harmful touch. Even when the touch is neutral, it startles me. Manicures and pedicures are especially difficult, and the technician is constantly telling me, "Relax your arms."

It's hard to relax when I'm being touched, even if it's something I signed up for.

Newborns need skin-to-skin contact in order to bond and grow. Skin, our largest organ, is both the sensor and protector of our body. So powerful is touch that, in fact, the physiological mechanisms of it have the capacity to impact our health outcomes positively. In a 2014 study published by the Association for Psychological Science,[1] touch was shown to bolster the immune systems of participants who had been exposed to the cold virus. After placing the participants in quarantine, researchers exposed them to the cold virus, after which 78 percent of the subjects were infected, with 30 percent showing symptoms of the sickness. Researchers then found that subjects who had experienced recent social interactions such as hugging or closeness prior to isolation exhibited fewer signs of illness or fought the infection more effectively.

David Linden, professor of neuroscience at Johns Hopkins University, writes in his book *Touch: The Science of the Hand, Heart, and Mind*, "Interpersonal touch is a crucial form of social glue. It can bind sexual partners into lasting couples. It reinforces bonds between parents and their children and between siblings. It connects people in the community and in the workplace, fostering emotions of gratitude, sympathy, and trust. People who are gently touched by a server in a restaurant tend to leave larger tips. Doctors who touch their patients are rated as more caring, and their patients have reduced stress-hormone levels and better medical outcomes. Even people with clipboards at the mall are more likely to get you to sign their petitions or take their surveys if they touch your arm lightly."[2]

So, what happens when, because of trauma, your brain and body outright reject touch?

An interesting thing about domestic violence agencies is that no one touches you without asking. It's like a known thing that you should not reach out for, grab, pull, or touch any of the survivors there for any reason, unless there is a fight or someone is in danger. And the reason I know this is because when I was greeted at the shelter—from the moment of intake to my first appointment with the domestic violence counselor—no one touched me. No one even asked to touch me. And I appreciated that because I don't think I wanted to be touched.

Surviving abuse did considerable damage to my sense of intimacy, and for a while I could not stand to be touched sexually or nonsexually. Every new person I met at work expected me to touch them. When I caught up with friends I hadn't seen in a long time, there were immediate hugs. I hated hugs because the feeling of two arms enveloping my body was like being trapped. I'd stopped being sexually intimate with H. a bit before I left the marriage, so by the time I was out in the world, touch felt unusual and unwanted.

And if you think about it, touching is strange. It is equal parts intrusive and necessary. We touch door handles in order to gain entry or make exit. We touch keyboards as we type. We touch our phones to browse or communicate with others. We wake up in the morning and touch everything in our bathrooms, from toilet paper to deodorant in order to get ready for our day. We put nails to skin in order to scratch away an itch, effectively bringing relief. We touch *everything* all the time without a second thought.

But then we also touch in order to express something. The touch could be an embrace to show affection, it could be a yank to keep a little child from danger, for instance, if they stepped out into a street without noticing a car was coming. It could be sensual like the moment you hold hands with someone you like, or that first kiss. It could be a handshake, a formality acknowledging people you work with or that you've just met, a desire to keep up with the appropriate business protocols. We touch so much, and after surviving I didn't want to touch anyone at all.

I quickly discovered that I also had an aversion to sudden moves. If someone jumped or raised their hand quickly, even to swat away a flying insect, it startled me. I didn't know what it meant, and I didn't know if that swing was coming my way. I needed everyone to be *very still* at all times, in a world where no one is still. It was a demand I was placing on the world that I knew would not be met. The cost for me being deep anxiety, with just the give-and-take of social interactions on a daily basis becoming too much.

The first time I had sex after leaving my marriage was in Chicago, with the owner of the home I was renting a room out of. This is not a sexual relationship I necessarily wanted to have. After a night out with friends, he asked if I would join him on the sofa to watch the movie *Love Jones*. I was tired, tipsy, and wanted to go to bed, but he was so insistent that I set my purse down and slid onto the sofa, as far away from him as possible.

I sat there, ready to watch that movie with him. I thought, "It's fine; it's just a movie. Plus, he's my landlord, I'm living in his house. I guess we should bond?" As a woman with no resources and little money, I felt unprotected in every way. H. had been my protector for so many years; I hadn't been out in the world alone for a long time. I didn't really know how to navigate except to rely on my instinct. The bigger problem is that I didn't start *listening* to that instinct until after this happened. Because my instinct said very clearly, "Run away!" but I still sat on the sofa to watch *Love Jones*, thinking that would be the safest action for me at that moment.

Almost immediately into the first scene, I knew he wanted to have sex with me. I knew that because he was talking through the entire first scene as opposed to watching it. His eyes focused squarely on my breasts.

"You said that he was abusive?"

"Yes," I said.

"Like, physically abusive? Did he hit you?"

"Yes," I said.

"Well, that's terrible, I'm sorry."

I didn't know whether to say "it's okay" in an effort to comfort him from his feelings of sorrow about my current situation or to remain silent about the whole thing. I decided to just remain silent with my eyes squarely on *Love Jones*.

But he started talking again.

"You know, I read something one time about touch," he said. "I read that people who get out of an abusive relationship have to experience a lot of positive touch. They've had so much negative touch that constant positive touch reinforces the goodness of others."

"That's interesting," I said. He scooted closer to me.

"Yeah so," he gently put my hand in his hand, rubbing my palm and tracing it with his fingers. "You have to seek out positive touch, you know? And when it comes, you just have to be ready for it. You have to really let it in," he continued.

"Uh-huh," I responded, hoping that if I kept staring at the television, he'd stop positive-touching me.

At this point in the story, you're probably expecting me to snatch my hand back from him, run upstairs, and lock my room door at this moment. I'm sorry to disappoint you if you expected that; I didn't. He continued to positive-touch my arm, which led to him grabbing the breasts that he'd been staring at for ten minutes and then kissing me. That led to sex on the couch, which I assume he was hoping would be a positive-touch experience as well.

It wasn't. The sex was just sex. It was quick and hurried, not sensual. Transactional. I wasn't into it and didn't provide any affirmative cues in the form of moans, or "yes," or "more," or any of the sexy things people say when they're enjoying positive touch. I was just present, waiting for it to be over so I could go to bed and write my email to him the next day, letting him know I was moving out.

But this chapter is not about the loss of my $845 security deposit that he refused to return to me.

The truth is, I didn't need to be touched positively; I needed to be *loved well*. I needed attention, not always sexual, but someone who would care for me and regularly check in about my wellbeing. I had not been loved well in a long time. No doubt that I had been loved. I believe that H. loved me. But I had not been loved in a way that made me feel free or inspired. What I needed, and what restored my joy of touch, was patience, gentleness, respect, and to be made to feel safe.

Throughout 2020, during the COVID-19 pandemic, I lived alone for more than a year without being touched. And a few months into the pandemic I began to crave hugs; I would wrap my arms firmly around myself just to mimic the feeling of being embraced. I think a lot about trauma and why people are so hesitant to name it, outside of situations like physical violence. Naming trauma assigns us an identity—something we have to then work through. And, just like the descriptor "victim," some people may consider trauma, or acknowledging trauma, to be weak.

COVID-19 was traumatic, and it made us think carefully about the nature of the workplace, hygiene, and personal space. Unemployment is traumatic, as it interrupts a flow of social interaction, isolating you in a financially desperate bubble. Rejection is traumatic, as the reality of being unwanted by someone you want can damage your self-esteem, making you question your self-worth. These are all traumas.

And mine was touching. Working through the issue of touch was hard, and at times I still struggle. But I'm going to explain four practices I've relied on to make it easier.

NEGOTIATE (AND RENEGOTIATE) YOUR BOUNDARIES

Developing boundaries happened for me late in life. I never knew boundaries as a child; my parents were always present, with no restrictions, whether I wanted them to be there or not, throughout my entire childhood. I was not encouraged to say "no" or "I don't like that"; those words were considered disrespectful in the home. And that impacts you growing up. While I felt comfortable drawing lines in terms of people outside of my home, lines were nonexistent for people *inside* of my home.

It took a therapist I worked with, when I was well past the age of thirty, to inform me that not only are boundaries essential; *boundaries are freedom.* When you create a boundary, you are saying, "We are free to engage, explore, and create right here, within these lines." And that is beautiful. Boundaries are not harmful or rude, quite the opposite. A clear boundary is an invitation to continue in relationship with someone, just on terms that are healthy for you.

A few of my touch boundaries have been: Not having others reach out to hug me without asking, "Can I hug you?" I also do the same in return with others. I even ask if it is okay to touch a person in any way, be it a fist bump or a pat on the back. Another boundary is, in intimacy, I remove my own clothes, or the person I'm with should ask if it's okay to remove my clothes. I'll rarely find myself in a "ripping off clothes" situation, unless I'm ripping them off of myself.

And some boundaries have changed over time, based on my comfort level. It's okay to renegotiate your boundaries, whenever a boundary feels outdated or irrelevant. That could mean removing a boundary, expanding a boundary, or creating a new boundary.

ASSERT YOUR NEEDS

I've found that knowing what you don't want is equally as important as knowing what you want. For instance, in professional life, I don't want direct reports. In dating, I don't want an unreliable partner. In food, I don't want added salt. In my home, I don't want shoes. In bodily autonomy, I don't want to give birth. In pie, I don't want cherries. Knowing each of these things helps me efficiently design my life and decide what will or won't be a part of it.

When you meet someone, or even begin dating someone, talk about your needs. Give as much detail as you want but be honest in what you share. Tell them what you like, want, and need. Talk about how touch feels to you; what feels good and what doesn't. Talk about sensory concerns or the speaking volume level. If relationship tension bothers you, explain why and come up with a strategy for dealing with tension, be it taking a one-hour break or talking through it.

The story of your survival is a huge plot-driver and, I believe, necessary for those who want to know you. While we shouldn't trust just anyone or everyone with the details of our lives, or our survival, once you are in community with another, I believe it's important for your health to express clearly and honestly who you are and what your needs are.

My needs are clear to me, and that makes them easy to assert. I need to see my partner at least once a week, or if they are long distance, twice a month. I need a partner who will text back when they're available, not a day or two later. I need brief check-ins in the form of short phone calls or text messages that say, "thinking of you" or "miss you." I need gentleness; I do not respond well to teasing or aggression. Don't make a derogatory joke because that will get you blocked. I need maturity, and I need to feel safe. More than anything else, *I need to feel safe.*

ACCEPT WHERE YOU ARE

As much as I wanted to move rapidly through the period of my life when I rejected touch, trying to do that caused even more pain. I was forcing myself into situations of touch, creating stress and tension in my body with every moment, thinking that if I was touched *a lot*, then eventually, I'd like it. But it took accepting where I was in whatever moment I found myself in—whether that was rejecting touch, accepting touch, or viewing touch as neutral—to find a measure of peace in that period of my life.

I read a beautiful book by Lama Rod Owens, a Buddhist teacher, called *Love and Rage: The Path of Liberation through Anger*. In it, he writes this about acceptance:

> Acceptance means simply allowing the thing to be there, whatever the thing is. It is a practice of no judgment. We are not interested in the quality or nature of the thing at the time. We are just interested in letting the thing be there. Of course, this brings us back to our work of holding space, which is still defined as allowing the thing to be there. Holding space means that we are both allowing and accepting something. Accepting without judgment means we are not celebrating or denying the thing. For example, I hurt my foot when I started writing this chapter. Though there was pain, the real inconvenience was losing full mobility of my foot. The thing was the pain I was experiencing. That was the basic experience of a sensation that was not pleasurable. The suffering of the situation was the added layer of resisting feeling this pain. My work was to hold space for the pain, which was again to accept the pain. When I was able to do this, then the pain became more ordinary and less of a distraction. I found myself less distracted and had the spaciousness to consider remedies like taking aspirin, icing my foot, staying off it, and massaging it. Acceptance offers us the space to develop wisdom, and it's from that wisdom space that we can decide how to address what we are holding space for.[3]

Accepting where I am in my healing journey creates room for me to explore my new needs in the space that I find myself. If I'm in a place, emotionally, where I can't handle the weight of constant communication with others, then I can accept that, take quick steps to assert that—that is, send a few text messages to loved ones to explain I'll be out of touch for a few days and not to worry—and then take the time I need to move through that space without the anxiety of feeling bad for not showing up in the lives of others. And remember that wherever you are, whatever space you find yourself in while healing, is *okay*. I'm going to keep saying that throughout this book. *You are okay.*

PAY ATTENTION TO YOUR REACTIONS

Everything is information, including how we react to people and situations. Those reactions can inform us about how we feel, how we're adjusting, what we need, and what we don't need.

One time I was dating this guy and I was really into him; we had a connection. We talked all day every day; it was comfortable and intense, but not rushed. He was very gentle with me and took time to get to know me over the course of a month or two. I was feeling very safe with him. I wanted to be touched by him, known by him, and I thought that he wanted to be known by me as well. But then, just as smoothly as he entered my life, he disappeared from it.

My initial reaction was genuine confusion and concern for his wellbeing, because we had been talking so regularly for a significant period of time that when he simply didn't call back, I thought something must be wrong. So out of concern (and nosiness), I went to his social media pages and refreshed them every hour or so, looking for signs of life. After a few hours of no posting or commenting, I started to get even more concerned. I called and left a message for him again. The phone rang a few times before going to voicemail, so at least I knew his phone was both charged and active. But I still hadn't heard from him. The next day, I went to refresh his social media account and noticed that he *had been* posting and commenting. That's when I realized I was being ghosted.

My next reaction was offense. I was offended! Not only that someone would get to know me intimately and not even show me basic respect by ending whatever situationship we had going on, but I was also offended that amid the ghosting process, he was sitting there publicly laughing and joking with other people! Eventually, offense transformed to anger. I don't do much with anger except work it out internally; I'm not someone who yells, fights, or argues. I simply deal with those feelings of anger via a conversation, or, if I've been ghosted, I just move on.

But all those reactions were *information* about me. I learned that my natural state of dealing with people is to assume the best. It did not cross my mind that he was ghosting me. What did cross my mind is that he might be hurt. But the next piece of information I gathered from the second reaction, offense, was that I deeply value respect and communication in a relationship, even if that relationship is ending.

While one of the challenges I had after surviving was touch, yours may be different. Or, you may have found that just the blessing of getting out alive removed many or all of the issues you faced when shifting from a place of abuse to one of freedom. In whatever state you find yourself, I hope you can accept who you are, where you are, while processing the information you're discovering about yourself.

Chapter 8

HARM REDUCTION

"The axe forgets but the tree remembers."
—African proverb

I was first diagnosed with PTSD (Post-Traumatic Stress Disorder) about one year after I left my marriage. I hadn't been sleeping, and I was having constant nightmares, trouble remembering simple things such as day-to-day events, and lots of flashbacks. Additionally, I started to have phantom pain all over my body. I didn't identify any of this as PTSD because PTSD was something I believed was reserved for combat veterans, or someone who survives a mass shooting. But surviving abuse is just as traumatic as both of those things.

The American Psychiatric Association defines Post-Traumatic Stress Disorder as "a psychiatric disorder that may occur in people who have experienced or witnessed a traumatic event such as a natural disaster, a serious accident, a terrorist act, war/combat, or rape or who have been threatened with death, sexual violence or serious injury."[1] The four categories that symptoms of PTSD fall in are intrusion, avoidance, alterations of cognition and mood, and alterations in arousal and reactivity. What I struggled with most was intrusion, in my case, the flashbacks that would freeze me in place because they felt so real in the moment, and the alterations in reactivity, that is, everything I described in the previous chapter—being on high alert regarding touch, fearing sudden movements, and being easily alarmed.

Although the specific ways trauma manifests in survivors is personal and subjective, many survivors of domestic violence experience symptoms of PTSD due to the distinctive experience of intimate partner violence as a traumatic event. Dr. Tanya Grant, a professor and researcher at Mercy College, wrote about the connection between domestic violence and PTSD. In her essay "PTSD and Domestic Violence," she explains,

> Interpersonal trauma has been found to be more strongly related to PTSD than most other traumatic events; accordingly, women who are victims of violence by an intimate partner have been found to be more likely to suffer from PTSD (Sullivan et al. 2009). Furthermore, domestic violence victims are often subjected to prolonged periods of physical abuse, psychological abuse, and sexual abuse. Unfortunately, studies are limited regarding a gauge of which type of abuse causes PTSD more frequently, especially since every victim is different and every incident uniquely impacts each victim. However, studies have definitively shown that psychological abuse increases the trauma of physical and sexual abuse, and a number of studies have demonstrated that psychological abuse alone causes long-term damage to a victim's mental health. In addition, women experiencing psychological abuse are significantly more likely to report poor physical and mental health and to have more than five physician visits in the past year (Coker et al. 2000). Moreover, studies have confirmed that psychological abuse is a stronger predictor of PTSD than physical abuse among women; seven out of ten psychologically abused women display symptoms of PTSD and/ or depression. [2]

I spent a lot of time minimizing the effects of the abuse, particularly the physical part of the abuse, on my body and mind. My near constant refrain was "I'm fine!" even when I wasn't. I carried a lot of survivor's guilt; I thought since I made it out alive, I had no right to present as suffering in any way. My life was a gift, and to walk around with anything less than joy and thankfulness was disrespect-ful to those who did not make it out alive. When I had nightmares, or body aches, or memories of both pain and happiness that brought me to tears, I dismissed those moments, because being alive was all that mattered. But it was not all that mattered. I was happy to be alive, yes, but I wanted to be alive *and well*.

So, when I was first given the PTSD diagnosis, I didn't really want to believe it. It felt like one more weight to carry—Why couldn't I just be free of the situation? At every turn it seemed like some new thing arrived to interrupt my life when all I really wanted was stasis. Peace. Maybe a margarita.

So, I started another new journey. It was a journey working through the trauma of the relationship and learning how to manage those traumas so that I could be a person in the world. I wanted to understand how to live with the trauma and symptoms that come with surviving abuse while still being able to have *healthy relation-ships* that don't cause harm to myself or others.

And I want to stop here for a moment because there's something that I want to make clear before we go on. Before I explain the ways that *I* caused harm after surviving abuse, I want to be clear that surviving abuse itself does not make you predisposed to doing harm. *You are not more likely to harm someone, physically or emotionally, simply because you experienced abuse.* In fact, according to the U.S. Department of Veterans Affairs, those in treatment or with a diagnosis of PTSD are more likely to engage in self-harm versus harming others.[3]

However, trauma can leave long-lasting scars that might com-pletely change your demeanor. I found that those changes, in my case, tilted toward an aversion to touch, close emotional contact, any level of vulnerability, and intense anger directed at anyone who was even slightly critical of me. And the concentrated combination of those things led to isolation, which led to loneliness, which led to feelings of helplessness.

So, this chapter is not about self-blame or criticism. This chapter is about how, after learning that some of my defensive behaviors in nonabusive relationships were hurtful to my partners, I had to look clearly and carefully at the ways surviving abuse led me to act in ways that were challenging for, or harmful to, dating partners.

I'll also explain some behaviors that are abusive, and if you are intentionally engaging in them, how you can reverse course.

UNINTENTIONAL HARM

Harm is different from abuse and can happen for many reasons, intentional and unintentional. First, I want to talk about unintentional harm. The things we do to protect ourselves from violence can be the same things that cause unintentional harm to family, friends, or people we date after the threat of violence is gone. I'm not going to tell you that causing harm is okay. It's not—and I think we all know that intuitively. But what we also know is that at times we cause harm without understanding the harm we've caused, or *why*. I choose to have a lot of grace with myself when realizing I've inadvertently hurt someone, and I hope you have the same grace for yourself if anything in this chapter feels familiar to you.

To douse my husband's temper, I'd withdraw, using days-long silence or sleeping in another room until it felt safe to re-engage. But when I started dating again, I'd withdraw using those same days-long silence any time there was a disagreement, even if we were both calm and there was no indication of danger.

It was a reflex. Some might say a coping mechanism. But to me, it was just the way relationships were: We argue or disagree, then we do not speak to each other until one of us breaks. It was *my normal*. But that did not mean it was normal. Multi-day silence in a relationship is unhealthy unless that is the agreed upon modus operandi of the relationship. But if you and your partner are usually in close, frequent contact throughout the day, then The Silent Treatment is unwelcome.

I can't say I even realized I was using the silent treatment as a defense-turned-weapon, that's how natural it came to me.

Some years back I was dating a guy who was kind, with a gentle nature and caring heart. I was super into him, mostly because he was hilarious and thoughtful. He was also emotionally solid and thrived in situations where we communicated clearly.

One day he said to me, "Why do you disappear?"

I was confused at first because I was sitting right next to him.

"What do you mean, babe?" I asked him.

"Like," he began. "Where do you go when you don't talk to me?"

I knew exactly what he meant at that point because we had just worked through a disagreement two weeks before.

Whenever we had an argument or just a basic disagreement that upset me, I brought up the thing that bothered me with him, in an effort to assert myself. But if he didn't respond by immediately apologizing, or if he wanted to have an extensive conversation about why I was upset, I would shut down.

"I don't go anywhere," I said. "I just keep to myself, real talk, I just stay away from you."

"Why?" he asked. "Why do you stay away from me? Why don't we just talk about it instead of being mad for two days and then ignoring it?"

"I don't know," I said to him.

This was a long-distance relationship, and I was living a few states away from him. The foundation of our very relationship was digital communication. We met online through friends that we had in common and spent a lot of time talking, so I was upset by his claim that I would disappear on him because I never did that. But as I thought about it, he was right. When a disagreement felt over-whelming, I checked out. The argument we had that time was so inconsequential that I can't even remember its origins. But I knew he wasn't wrong, and I had no intention of gaslighting him.

One thing that I've always been good at is getting off the phone or just basically removing myself from an argument when I feel like it's going nowhere. Not to say that I'll never come back to it, but I'm not someone who is going to continue an argument or disagree-ment when I'm not sure that we can reach a resolution. When we had the disagreement two weeks prior to this conversation, after arguing for a few minutes I got off the phone with him—my standard way of dealing with tension. But then I didn't talk to him . . . for the next two days.

Now, I could claim that it wasn't intentional for me not to talk to him for the next two days, but, in truth, it was. I was upset by what he said to me, I was upset by his opinion on whatever we were arguing about, and I decided that I didn't want to talk to him.

But that hurt him, particularly because he was so into effective communication. So while I'm thinking, "Let me get some space," he was thinking, "She abandoned me."

I had no idea, at the time, why that behavior seemed right and came so naturally to me. So, of course, I went straight to Google.

I learned about two specific behaviors I frequently engaged in that made personal relationships difficult. And again, these behaviors are specific to me and the ways that I caused harm while beginning my healing journey. While they might not apply to you, I hope you might take something from the lessons I've learned.

STONEWALLING

Stonewalling became a relationship behavior of mine that was harmful outside of the context of abuse. If a dating partner upset me, or if I felt any tension in the relationship, I'd shut down and avoid them completely—often for days at a time. And I had my reasons. It was easier for me not to face conflict, because for me, conflict meant the potential for violence. So, I just detached altogether. But that was not the healthiest way to handle conflict, and it was unfair to my dating partner who rightfully hoped I'd be open and vulnerable with them.

But vulnerability, to me, meant *danger*. Trauma can make you behave in ways that are unfamiliar to those who know you best.

Of stonewalling, psychotherapist Marni Feuerman writes this:

Stonewalling involves refusing to communicate with another person. Intentionally shutting down during an argument, also known as the silent treatment, can be hurtful, frustrating, and harmful to the relationship. Stonewalling is broadly described by the following behaviors: a general discomfort in discussing feelings, dismissing or minimizing a partner's concerns, refusing to respond to questions, refusing to make eye contact or offer nonverbal communication cues, walking away from discussions that cause stress. While stonewalling can be hurtful, you shouldn't necessarily assume that it is inherently ill-intended. At its very heart, stonewalling is often a behavior born out of fear, anxiety, and frustration.[4]

I am in the walking-away-from-discussions-that-cause-stress camp. And I like that Feurerman wrote that while hurtful, stonewalling may not be "ill-intended," because many survivors I speak with engage in some form of stonewalling behavior, and the thing we all have in common is that we believe we are *protecting ourselves from potential danger*.

Feuerman continues:

There are a few different ways that stonewalling might appear in a relationship. These include:

Unintentional stonewalling: Sometimes stonewalling is a learned response that partners use to cope with difficult or emotional issues. People who stonewall may do so to avoid escalating a fight or to avoid discussing an uncomfortable topic. They also might be afraid of their partner's reaction.

Intentional stonewalling: In extreme cases, stonewalling is used to manipulate a situation, maintain control in the relationship, or inflict punishment. If you think your partner is verbally abusing you, speak with a counselor or therapist for advice.

Behaviors that are mistaken for stonewalling: It's important to note that stonewalling is not the same thing as asking for space or setting boundaries. Asking for time or space requires communication. When partners ask if they can discuss something later, they are not stonewalling you. In fact, insisting that they speak to you at that moment when they have asked for space is controlling.

HYPERVIGILANCE

After I left H., I knew I wouldn't be able to date for a while. I was sensitive because I was at the very beginning of healing, but I was also combative and inflexible. I couldn't imagine taking part in the daily negotiations that are a part of any healthy relationship. I hated the thought of making compromises. I'd made so many in my marriage that all I wanted was to accommodate myself only.

I was hypervigilant, always. Hypervigilance is a heightened state of excessive alertness and stress that can cause severe emotional reactions, stress on the body from the relentless state of being in flight-or-fight mode and the need to assess the risk of threats around you constantly. This persistent state of fear made it difficult to establish new, healthy relationships.

In daily life, hypervigilance showed up in everyday interactions. If someone was walking toward me, I tensed up, ready to fight if necessary. When they walked past me, I would look over my shoulder to make sure they hadn't doubled back to follow me.

In dating, I was always looking for that person to mess up in some way, just constantly anticipating bad things. In a perpetual state of waiting for the other shoe to drop—and sometimes, it did! A lot of times, actually. I've been with people who lied about being married or about having a child on the way. Men who stalked me once it was over. I've dated people who said they wanted me but chose someone else. My heart is littered with ashes from small fires I've set trying to destroy the achy memories of men who did not choose me.

But I've also been so hypervigilant that I turned down or rejected partners that meant me no harm. I was talking to my therapist once about possibly going on a date with someone I liked. My first concern, I explained to her, was that he just wanted sex.

"How do you know that he just wants sex?" she asked.

"I don't know," I said. "But what if they do? Then I've wasted time, makeup, and gas when I could've been watching TV."

She laughed. "I want you to consider something. Are you ready?"

I wasn't, but okay.

"Yes," I replied.

"I want you to consider that he might want to go on a date with you to get to know you, and that's all."

I thought for a minute. "But what if that's not all?"

"What if it is?"

I sat there, side-eyeing her.

"I just want you to think about that. What if you have fun? What if he doesn't try to sleep with you, but gives you a hug and says goodnight? What if you enjoy the evening with him? Just consider that."

I won't leave you wondering for long; I did not go on the date (it's okay to laugh). I couldn't go! My hypervigilance took over and I could not get comfortable with the idea that joy was a potential outcome as opposed to more pain. But that gave me something to work with. *What if he meant me no harm?* How much more relaxed might I be moving throughout my day with the expectation that harm will not come to me, that someone in my life wants goodness for me and not pain? The thought of it makes me feel good. And hopefully I'll get there one day. Right now, I'm balancing my hypervigilance with the idea that it could be less prominent in my life. We'll see where my healing journey takes me from here.

There have been quite a few times in my life following abuse that I've intended to show up fully in a relationship and just could not do that. For whatever reason, well, for many reasons, I would try to access the best version of myself for this new potential love and fall flat. And if I wasn't falling flat, I was being hurtful in some way.

And sometimes I knew I was being hurtful—not violent—and it just was what it was, you know? I felt like this new person had to prove to me that they were good and not bad, kind and not mean, gentle and not rough. I led with distrust and suspicion, and it wore heavy on my soul. It's hard to start a new relationship after experiencing a relationship that didn't work out, but I think it's even more complicated to start a new relationship after surviving abuse. The fear of danger is there. The heartache is there. The memories of a love suddenly becoming violent are there. And what do you do with those memories? Most times I internalized them, tried to bulldoze my way through the world, ignoring the signals my mind, body, and spirit were giving me to pause, rest, and reassess.

Self-soothing techniques ease my stress and have helped me reduce the tendency to stonewall and be hypervigilant. Practices such as deep, slow breathing when I feel anxious, or drinking a warm cup of tea to help invite calmness. Aromatherapy is also a regular presence in my home; I have various scents all around. I like to put a different scent in each room, so that walking around the house is like a scent journey with every step. In the bedroom, I'm surrounded by lavender. In the bathroom, I like a powdery scent or a vanilla. In the living room I usually have a tobacco or warm amber. In the kitchen, a citrus scent. In the hallway, a floral scent. When I'm stressed, I can take a walk through my home and detach in a healthy way, taking in the different scents and allowing my imagination to help me escape the moment. And when I'm ready, I return to reality.

Warm baths or showers also soothe me. Followed by body oils, and nature sounds while lying in bed. The goal, for me, is to intentionally engage several of my senses so that they can work in tandem to heal me.

There's that saying, "hurt people hurt people." I've always disliked that saying, because I don't like giving hurt people an identity of being someone who is going to cause harm. I know plenty of hurt people who don't hurt people. They may hurt themselves; they may think about the hurt they've experienced. But they don't hurt other people. I was not one of those people though; I hurt people, and it's something that I carry with me. It's not weighty, but it's there; knowing that there are people who have experienced the worst parts of me makes me sad at times. And they might not ever forgive me, even if I'm sorry, and I believe that's their choice. But going forward, I hope to live a conscious life, being aware of my tender spots, and to work hard to make sure that the tender spots don't become tender spots for others.

There were moments when, in hurt or frustration, I intentionally said or did something harmful to someone I was in a romantic relationship with. And I need to confess that here, so that you don't leave this book thinking that I have moved through life solely as the wounded and never the wound-maker. The wounds I've caused, while never physical, have been emotional or psychological.

In late 2012, I started dating a guy who I'd met through some friends. He lived in Detroit; I lived in Chicago. So, whenever we got a chance to see each other it was like a vacation—a romantic rendezvous twice a month. A lot of kissing, a lot of handholding, and a lot of lovemaking.

We always used condoms, but on one of these trips where we'd met halfway, neither of us had an available condom. We'd been dating a few months and both felt safe in this committed relationship, so we went without one. The following morning, we picked up a Plan B pill from the grocery store; I took it, and that was that.

A few weeks later I missed my period. I was working at a health clinic at the time, and I remember telling my friend, a nurse there, about my missed period.

"Do you wanna take a test?"

"No," I said. I wanted to wait and see if it would arrive. It was winter holiday season, and the stress of holidays might have made me late.

"You know you need to take a test," she continued.

"I'll take one next week," I said, sharply. In that tone you speak in when the conversation is over or should be.

A week later, my period hadn't shown up, and I was nauseous. I walked through the feet-high Chicago snow to the drugstore nearby and got two of the cheapest pregnancy tests I could find. Two positive tests later, I called my partner to tell him that I was pregnant.

"No," he said. "No, no, no."

My partner was recently divorced with two kids already. He'd been clear from the beginning that he had no interest in having more children, and I was fine with that as I was, at the time, undecided. But the way he was reacting to the news pissed me off.

"What do you mean, 'no'?" I asked.

"You took a Plan B! Did you take the pill?" he asked.

"Of course I took the pill. Do you think I *want* to be pregnant right now?"

"I don't know what you want," he said, transforming into someone I did not like. "All I know is that you cannot have this baby."

And I took that personally. Here, a man with two children, was telling me that having a baby with me was unacceptable?

"What's wrong with having a baby with me?" I asked.

"You know that's not it," he responded. "I don't want another kid right now. I have kids already, and they're enough."

I started to cry.

"I hate your kids," I said. I knew what I was saying, and I knew it was a terrible thing to say. I knew it would hurt him. And to this day, I deeply regret saying those words.

"What did you say?" he yelled. "You hate my kids? You don't even know my kids! Why would you say something like that?"

"Because you want your kids, but you don't want mine, as if my kid isn't good enough for you!" I yelled back.

He sat silently on the phone, and I couldn't tell if he was stunned or just done with me. After about a minute of silence, I said goodbye and hung up the phone.

I didn't hate his kids. I had never even met his kids. What I hated was that they could be a source of joy and pride for him but mine would not.

Two days later, I began to bleed a little. The day after that, I began to bleed a lot. I had miscarried.

To his credit, he was kind to me throughout the miscarriage process—he went with me to the clinic to get the pills that would expel the gestational sac from my uterus, and he paid for the treatment. Our relationship ended there, and while we've spoken briefly over the years, and I apologized for what I said, I don't know that my apology helped mend that wound.

There have been other situations where I behaved poorly or said harmful words, and healing the deep regret I have had for causing those harms has been a unique journey. For me, it has meant recognizing my words or actions as damaging, admitting that I've been a harm-doer, exploring the metaphorical weapons that I used, and asking for help in order to act differently in the future. And I hope my journey helps you if you've also done harm. Know that harm is caused by all of us, intentional and unintentional, and the best thing we can do once we have recognized it is to take responsibility for it and put in the work needed to change the parts of us that are liable for those harms.

WHEN BEHAVIORS ARE ABUSIVE

While I was speaking at a college a few years ago, a young woman walked up to me after the lecture.

"I wanted to ask you a question," she said. "What if you think you might be doing the abuse? Like, you're the one that's emotionally abusive?"

I don't get this question often, but it touches on a problem that the domestic violence movement faces: How do we confront abuse when so many of us see it, or the potential for it, in ourselves?

In my experience, abusers know or *perceive* that they are abusing. They might not have the terms for it, or they may deny it, but that denial is for self-preservation only. Abusers know that what they are doing is very damaging. Abuse is on purpose. When intentional harm is a pattern—prolonged or done systematically—with the intention to create a power dynamic in which you maintain that power throughout the relationship, you have crossed over into abuse.

Part of the complexity of domestic violence is that at any moment, in any relationship, we could be the abusive one *if we choose to be*. If we expand our view to include emotional, financial, and

psychological violence in the standard accepted definition of intimate partner violence, then we might notice the behaviors in ourselves. For example, a time you secretly go through your partner's
phone without their permission. When you keep tabs on their movement via Snapchat maps without telling them that you know where
they are. When you made an "if you love me, you will . . ." statement with the intention of manipulating them into bending to your
will. All of these are examples of abusive behavior that are not
physical.

Often, I'll see articles or tweets asking why the issue of domestic
violence doesn't seem to get as much attention as other social issues, and my opinion is this: Domestic violence is the one issue that
is so insidious that when we see it in ourselves, it frightens us into
silence. Because if we come face to face with all the different types
of abuse, we must then face ourselves. And that is our true fear.

Just think: When a story about intimate partner violence among
celebrities makes headlines, within the hour there will be people
saying, "But they were so nice to me!" Otherwise rational people
will make statements claiming an abuser isn't abusive because the
abuser bought them a latte once. But to me, that demonstrates how
close we all are to the issue of domestic violence, how people we
cherish may abuse in some way, or we may be abusive ourselves.

So when behaviors are not unintentional harm, when the behaviors are abuse, what can you do?

The team at the National Domestic Violence Hotline has this to
say on their website:

> People change. That small, two-word sentence is actually a
> huge, significant statement that carries a lot of weight. We grow
> up learning about change—the inevitability of it, the uncertainty
> it can bring. We change—our opinions, personalities, careers,
> friends and much more. Some changes feel like they happen
> overnight. Others are more conscious, and they have to be, like
> overcoming an addiction or correcting a personality flaw that's
> harmful to ourselves or others. While people do have the capac-
> ity to change, they need to want to deeply and be committed to

all aspects of change in order to begin to do so—and even then, it's a lot easier said than done.

In discussing why abusers abuse, it's clear that a lot of the causal factors behind these behaviors are learned attitudes and feelings of entitlement and privilege—which can be extremely difficult to change truly. Because of this, there's a very low percentage of abusers who truly do change their ways. One part of changing may involve an abusive partner willingly attending a certified intervention program that focuses on behavior, reflection, and accountability.[5]

Some years after I left my marriage, I received an email from H. In it, he shared a song he'd written and a poem. He apologized for everything that he did and said that he had changed. Since there wasn't a specific "let's talk" or "let's meet up" request in the email, I've always assumed his intention was not to get back together, but just to let me know he was sorry.

I don't know if H. has changed. I hope he has changed, and I hope no one after me experienced abuse. But what I do know is that I've spent the years that follow unlearning the defense mechanisms that kept me emotionally, and at times physically, safe from him, because those mechanisms are not helpful anymore. Moving forward, my hope for myself is that I stay grounded, watchful, careful, and confident in the new approaches—that I am continuously developing—to keep me safe while remaining compassionate to others.

Chapter 9

TOOLS FOR HEALING

"Healing is a process that requires practice."
—Darian Symoné Harvin

Healing is perpetual. By that, I mean healing is not a destination that you get to before you can make it in life. Rather, healing is perennial. Healing is a process. Healing is a natural part of life.

One of the reasons that I've always ignored healing as a destination or target is because I've never quite reached it, though I know I've experienced significant growth and change since leaving that marriage. But every now and then, meaning every few months or years, I have a moment that feels very similar to the terror I felt while living in an abusive relationship. Once, I walked by someone who was wearing the exact cologne H. used to wear, and that sent me into a spiral for hours. Another time, I was watching a film scene where a guy throws his wife against a wall, and I had to turn it off. I could not stomach it and had trouble sleeping that night. Does that mean I haven't healed at all? I don't think so. To me, it means that healing is still with me—that healing is ever present.

I think about this specific paragraph in Carmen Maria Machado's memoir *In the Dream House* a lot:

Nonstalgia (noun): The unsettling sensation that you are never able to fully access the past; that once you are departed from an event, some essential quality of it is lost forever. A reminder to remember: just because the sharpness of the sadness has faded does not mean that it was not, once, terrible. It means only that time and space, creatures of infinite girth and tenderness, have stepped between the two of you, and they are keeping you safe as they were once unable to.[1]

That concept of time and space as safety is meaningful if you consider the old saying, "time heals all wounds." Now, I don't necessarily think that's true, that time heals *all* wounds. Some, yes. But I think time has a way of busying our lives so that the pain of our wounds is less focal. Time builds us a bridge, separating our present life from former, but our former life is still visible and accessible, and its effects can be lasting. But time *itself* won't heal wounds, just like time itself hasn't healed the generational trauma of the enslavement of Black people in the United States, especially considering how policies and systems in this country are meant to remind us that we were once, and remain, disposable. Time hasn't healed that. But I do lean toward Machado's interpretation of time as a buffer between trauma and the memory of it.

Which then begs the question: How do you heal from abuse trauma if time and space don't automatically fade the effects away?

My answer to that is this: Develop a personalized toolbox tailored to your specific needs and open that toolbox to perform repairs, improvements, or tweaks as needed.

You know how medical professionals will tell you that you need to drink sixty-four ounces of water every day? That's how I view healing. Healing is something that I take part in every day. It's part exercise and part sustenance.

I want you to become comfortable with the idea that you might be healing *forever*. I am *constantly* healing. Healing is not a destination for me, it is something I carry with me along the journey. So healing is not the journey, *living is*. Healing accompanies me on that path, reminding me of the need to slow down or speed up, signaling discomfort in tender spots that need some attention under the hood, urging me to pause and pull over for a break at a rest stop. In some ways you may find parts of yourself that require healing at different moments, for instance, at times I need to heal my mind, particularly when it comes to nightmares and painful memories of the relationship.

At other times, I need to heal my heart when it comes to the heartbreak of choosing not to be with someone who I loved, and the difficulty in finding new love being the reinvented person that I am. And other times I need to heal myself sexually, learning not to use sex as an escape from what I'm feeling, but to engage in sex as pleasure when it feels good to me, and when I want to be completely present in that act.

There are so many tools for healing that I've discovered throughout this decade-long path, and I'm going to walk through the ones that I find myself circling back to regularly.

ANCHOR YOURSELF IN THE PRESENT

The nightmares don't come as frequently now, but I used to have them often. When I did, when I would wake up from that nightmare, I would force my eyes open, lift myself out of bed, put my feet on the floor, and feel either the carpet or the wood beneath them. Then I would stand up. Next, I would spread my arms to the side reaching for the walls without being able to touch them, but knowing they're there. In the darkness, I looked around, waiting for my eyes to focus on something in the room: an alarm clock, a night light, a candle, a crack of light coming from the hall. And when my eyes finally adjusted to something in the room, I would open my mouth and say, out loud, "I am here now. I am safe now." That practice is for anchoring yourself in the present.

Saying aloud: "I am here now. I am safe now."

It's a declaration, but it's also a command to your mind and spirit.

"I am here now. I am safe now."

Meaning, I'm not where I was. I'm not in the situation I was in that was unsafe. I exist, I am breathing, and I am okay.

If you are a person living with visual or mobility differences, or any disability that would make this anchoring exercise difficult, I encourage you to tailor it to your own needs. For example, as opposed to standing, you might relax into a position that makes you comfortable. Instead of focusing your sight on something in the room, you might begin to make soft sounds such as humming or clicking your tongue. The goal is to remind yourself that you are living in the present, and the past is not here with you.

REJECT A HEALING TIMETABLE

When people ask me how long it took to heal from abuse, I tell them that I am still, and will always be, healing from abuse. There is no healing deadline. Something I've noticed about modern-day wellness is that there is a distinctive focus on the *achievement* of healing, a definitive healing target. And if you don't reach that benchmark, if you are still angry, bitter, afraid, anxious, hesitant, or withdrawn after a certain amount of time has passed since the trauma, then something is wrong with you. You need to try a little harder, go a little bit deeper inside yourself. Buy a $50 candle, some organic soothing tea, and meditate until you transcend anger, catching up with the people who are dwelling in the realm of eternal peace.

I am not living in the realm of eternal peace, and trust me, neither is anyone else. What I am living in, is grace. A grace that is firmly rooted in the truth that life can be messy, a heart doesn't always feel what you want it to, minds can shuffle around the basement of the memory house, and everything, including healing, happens in waves.

I've actually been married twice; I married my second husband in 2013, just a few years after leaving the abusive marriage. My second husband was a gentle man who loved me deeply, and I loved him in the same way. He was not like H. in that he did not have a noticeable temper; I can count on one hand the number of times he got angry with me, and when he did, he sat down to quietly discuss the issue. And I loved that about him. I felt safe; I knew I could express myself fully and he would not react violently.

We got married after dating for three months. But I was not ready to be a spouse again as evidenced by my frequent need to run away—traveling to a cabin in the North Carolina mountains for days or deciding to move out for a few months to take a health policy course without discussing it with him—and after a while, that became clear to both of us.

While my second husband and I were separated, he fell in love with and got engaged to his second wife; he was already planning his next wedding before we'd even filed for divorce. And this is why healing is subjective. Because as of the moment I write this, years after my second marriage ended, I'm still unsure today if I'll ever remarry again. Was his healing process faster than mine? Or is the truth that healing is a route, a pathway, but not a destination?

I reject timetables in other ways as well. Many people without kids are regularly nudged by nosy family and friends, asking when they'll get started having children. Most single adults have had the experience of someone asking when they're going to "settle down," as if singleness is not a whole state in itself. We won't get into the theory of a biological clock here, particularly because clocks are so yesterday. But you get my point. Timetables are not for those who choose to live freely, without limitations. And for those of us who have survived abuse, freedom is our new life path.

I said all of that to say this: Don't pressure yourself to heal. Healing is a part of nature like rain. It occurs as it sees fit. Sometimes, it doesn't happen. A healing drought, if you will. But then suddenly it comes, nourishing as it falls, washing muck away. Sometimes it can feel like flooding, particularly when it is nonstop. But then it fades and recedes, leaving behind either clear skies or devastated lands. Who knows? All we know is that eventually it will come again, and again.

CHOOSE TO FEEL

Immediately after I left my abusive marriage, I cried for months. I felt like a failure. I felt every negative emotion and constantly projected them onto myself, sometimes without the help of others. But I'm thankful that I cried so much, for so long, because I wanted to feel the pain. I wanted to feel every ounce of that relationship seep from my body, and when the pain subsided, I felt better. And I don't regret feeling the pain instead of numbing it because I can see how that made me stronger.

Sometimes, after being hurt, we bury the pain. This burying is well intended; we do it to try and guard ourselves from additional pain, or worse, embarrassment. We put on so much armor, build so many walls, that our softness—the tenderness that has been with us since we cried out first tears at birth—is completely hidden. At times, we remove that armor, maybe just the helmet, definitely not the breastplate shielding our heart. But if hurt seems close by, we quickly put it all on again and go back into hiding.

This time, I chose not to hide. I chose not to numb; I wanted everyone in my life to know that I was fragile. The fragility, that pliable softness in my soul, created two things: physical relief from years of hiding my emotions out of fear of danger, and the opportunity to be vulnerable with others in the way that kinship requires.

Vulnerability is a tool for healing. *Choose to feel and be open about it.* You know when you've been busy all day, finally collapse into bed, but then stay up late, playing around on your phone or scrolling through Instagram? You wait until your body literally forces you to go to sleep and then finally, rest. But just as soon as you go to sleep, it's time to wake up the next day. And now here you are, awake. Exhausted, regretful, and expected to perform your daily duties in the new day. When, if you'd simply gone to sleep the night before and gotten the necessary rest, you would have been fine.

Choosing to feel is a lot like that. Avoiding the hard parts of what we're experiencing will make for really difficult days. We'll be cranky and irritable, unable to show up and perform. And truthfully, you can only go on for so long until something inside of you falls off the shelf, as Zora Neale Hurston writes. Choose to feel early and choose to feel as often as your heart needs.

In the early stages of life after abuse, I was part of group therapy at a local women's center. There were about eight to ten people in my group, and we met every Thursday to talk about anything at all, sometimes nothing. Not everyone in the group had similar experiences that brought them to this therapy—the only thread between us all was divorce.

But fairly quickly, a few women disclosed that they had experienced abuse in their marriages. One of them, an older woman with adult kids, once said, "I don't get sad."

"No?" asked the group counselor.

"Nah, I don't need that negativity," she said.

"Why do you think sadness is negative?" the counselor asked.

"I don't know, it takes me to a bad place in my head. I don't wanna be sad, I wanna be happy."

"Okay," said the counselor. "Could you tell us about the bad places sadness takes you to whenever you feel it?"

She sat there for a minute, and in her eyes, you could see the struggle to decide whether to, in that moment, access the sadness for us.

"My kids are grown now, see. And they spent they whole life watching they daddy beat me up. Twenty-two years he beat me up, and they saw it. They saw me spend all that time crying and carrying on, and I know they cried too. So now I'm gone, right? I'm gone, they gone and in college, so what I got to cry for? Crying makes me feel like I'm there in that bad place again. I don't have no good reason to cry now. Crying is for folks who wanna feel bad again. I don't wanna ever feel bad again."

I think about her words sometimes. The counselor didn't challenge her then, and I'm glad because I don't think it's always our place to tell others exactly how to process grief. But I suspect that her choice not to feel was not only a coping mechanism but also a security blanket. Her blanket was a smile or a neutral expression, but never a tear. And I get it. And I pray that that method of coping has worked well for her or that she found another way.

But for me, crying is not indicative of a place in time, and sadness is not negative. Sadness, and what it produces in me, are *signals that my heart still works*. That it is meaty and supple. That it remembers and knows and sees and perceives. That it still has the capacity to produce life. That it has the willingness to keep trying, loving, and seeking.

DESIGN YOUR COMMUNITIES

I always wanted to be low-key on Twitter. I remember signing up for Twitter right around the time I started to research domestic violence secretly on my computer when H. was at work. I don't remember exactly why I signed up for a Twitter account, but it seemed like a good thing to do in connection with reinventing my life. In fact, my first Twitter name was a play on the word "inventor."

But that account sat dormant for a few months while I built up my courage and executed my plan to leave the marriage. I checked in every now and then, but back in 2010 Twitter was not what it is today. It was a place that people went to shoot the shit, to talk about literally nothing and everything at the same time.

But before I get to why I became active on Twitter, I want to tell you about the most exciting part of my healing process: meeting new people. Meeting new people and making new friends is healing because community is a gateway to new life. We can only survive so long without community; I believe we are built to connect deeply with others and that those connections are vital to both our health and safety. Meeting new people is something H. never allowed me to do without his oversight. Every new person I met, regardless of where I met them, even if it was in church, had to be approved by H. After I left H. I returned to the original me, the me who loves people, loves exploring and learning about people, the me who is super curious about everything and wants to live life in various communities.

And I say various communities because being in more than one community is good for the soul. And I mean that. You are not one person, and one person only; you contain multitudes! And not every friend group will meet all of your needs. I've heard people say that they have their small circle of friends, two or three people, and those people are everything. I'm not like that, and I don't necessarily think that would work for me. I have several friend groups and all of them contribute something different to my life. I hope I contribute something different to theirs.

I have a friend group that I met from Twitter—six women and a non-binary friend—who I trust with the deepest parts of me. Over the last decade we've watched each other grow and change, take vacations together, get married, raise children, watch children graduate from high school, experience heartbreak, find new lovers, and have new sexual experiences. I learn so much from them because the relationship we have is based on respect and love, so they are never afraid to tell me when I'm wrong. I've learned about sensitive subjects like queer theory and rape culture, and cool topics like archaeology and supply chain planning. That group of friends is my lifeblood.

I have another group of friends who I consider my churchy friends. We all grew up knee deep in the Black church and speak a language that only folks who grew up like us would understand ("Amen, lights!"). If I say something about a Hammond organ, Richard Smallwood, or the COGIC bun, I know it won't be lost on them.

Another group of friends is a much smaller group. I consider them my sisters, because we are so close that they are truly a part of my family. What I love most about them is that we can go a significant amount of time without speaking to each other, but when we do there are no hard feelings or questions, just love. We're all introverts and we understand each other's need for space and time. When we do get together it's all laughs, hugs, mess, and pure joy.

I have another group of friends, actually just two guys, and being in community with them is so valuable. I listen to them have conversations about masculinity, dating, being Black men here in the U.S., and the unique challenges they face going through daily life. I've celebrated them getting new jobs and buying new cars, watched their younger siblings grow up, and seen them find themselves. And I feel comfortable sharing parts of myself with them, knowing that they will listen actively.

Before activism, before writing, before everything that people know me for now, I was a musician. *Music is my air.* I wake up in the morning and can't go five minutes without hearing some sound. I turn on music, ambient noises, anything that creates sound. And then I make my black tea.

Of the many things I love about my family, our deep involvement in and pleasure with music is one of the most important. Nearly everyone in my family can sing, and everyone in my family loves music. My brother loves music so much that he majored in music performance at Morgan State University and played piano—from classical to jazz—internationally. My ex-husband, H., was a musician.

After I left my marriage, I wanted to talk about music and nothing else. Back then I was only active on Facebook, so I would start music conversations there. But I wouldn't get much feedback; people weren't really into talking about music on Facebook. I'd reconnected with some old friends that I knew from Hampton University on Facebook too. It was one of these friends, Lawrence Cosby, who told me about the fun of Twitter.

After one of my unsuccessful attempts to get people to have a music conversation, Lawrence sent me a Facebook message:

"You should join Twitter!" he wrote.

"I think I have a Twitter account! But I don't wanna talk to strangers right now lol." (I genuinely believed Twitter was all about talking to strangers, and I have not been wrong about that.)

"No, it's fun and people are cool there! Just tweet your music opinion and people talk to you. I do it all the time."

I was skeptical of this, but then I was like, "Hey, why not?" I was anonymous on Twitter, and nobody knew who I was except for Lawrence. So, I tried it. I reset my password on Twitter and sent what would be my first music tweet. I wish I could tell you what the tweet said, but I have no idea at this point. All I know is that Lawrence responded to it, and then a whole lot of other people responded to it too, and by a whole lot I mean maybe ten, but again, this was 2010 Twitter.

And that, surprisingly, is the real reason I joined Twitter. Work-wise, I had moved from community organizing to corporate America and back, so I wasn't professionally focused on building as an activist on Twitter, although I would occasionally tweet about the social issues that were important to me, particularly issues surrounding housing and redlining. I'd occasionally tweet about organizing in Chicago where I lived at the time, and when Trayvon Martin was murdered, I used Twitter to cry openly about racism and get information on the local rallies to attend in support of the organizers and activists doing that work in Chicago.

Twitter can be used for whatever you want. The beauty of having an individual social platform is that you can be a chameleon and blend in with whatever topic is important to you, or you can choose to stand out and build a brand if you fashion yourself as a leader in some way, for instance in politics, journalism, or skincare. You can do none of that and show up anonymously—hopefully not to target and harass people—to seek out something that will fulfill you. You can engage with informational tools like hashtags and threads, and maybe even create your own.

The hashtag #WhyIStayed was born of raw emotion. It was a scream from my heart, a clarion call to readers to listen closely and judge never. Intended for a few, it circled the world, reaching 689 million Twitter users.[2] And through those three words I found even more community.

In order to meet new people, find friends and build an authentic community, you have to begin. *You have to be open to being seen.* Being open is hard, scary, even unpredictable. Let no one tell you that being open is easy; it is particularly difficult for survivors. But some of the most impactful relationships I've had, and the very reason I've been given the opportunity to write this book, is because in 2014, I showed up—open to being seen. And I believe you can do it too.

One caveat, though, is that social media is often used by abusers to monitor the activity and conversations of victims and survivors. While being active and engaging on social media can build community and a sense of belonging, it's also important to just be aware of how these sites can be used as tools of harm.

THOUGHTS ON FORGIVENESS

Forgiveness is a touchy concept for me. After the 2016 election, for example, we watched as Donald Trump said and did destructive things specifically to marginalized groups, such as immigrants and people of color. It seemed like the ink would barely be dry on whatever harmful executive order he'd just announced and immediately people would be calling for peace and forgiveness on Twitter. Forgiveness? For what?

It's inarguable, at this point in time, that Trump encouraged White supremacy and made racist remarks, particularly during the summer of 2020 when Black Americans protested the murder of George Floyd. But, if you take the word of religious leaders, political influencers, and even some citizens on the left, those who were the target of his daggers should grant him a pardon for his words *and* deeds.

I'm not going to do that, and I mean ever.

Forgiveness as virtue is flawed. I don't forgive solely to be forgiven because that reads as manipulative to me. I *hope* to be forgiven by others, not to secure my place in heaven, but because others chose to forgive me. And I don't lose sleep over this; this is not something I am trying to change about myself. There are people who I'll never forgive, and it is just fine. As far as I can tell, they are living happy, fulfilling lives without my pardon.

Forgiveness without remorse or atonement is what Adam Clayton Powell called "cheap grace,"[3] extending forgiveness to someone without the expectation of significant transformation. Further, some people use restorative terms like "reconciliation" or "mercy" as biblical encouragement to remain in dangerous relationships.

I believe in restoration, and I believe in reconciliation. But only if regret, apology, reflection, accountability, and *change* precede them.

We have a society of people trying so hard to forgive because we've convinced them that forgiveness is the path to peace, instead of dealing with the residual effects of the initial trauma itself. Forgiveness is absolutely a gift for the person who committed harm. And so withholding forgiveness, whether temporarily or permanently, does not make you an evil person, nor does it prevent you from living a positive, peaceful life. Peace does not require absolution. Forgiveness is *your* gift to give, or reserve.

Healing and moving on is possible without the exercise of forgiveness; forgiveness isn't a prerequisite to progress. The one person who I believe should always be forgiven by you, is you. I am constantly holding myself accountable, looking back on choices I've made, and choosing to grant myself the gift of my own forgiveness. And, if the harm I cause is external, meaning, if I've done harm to someone else and not just myself, I will ask for forgiveness, hope for it, *work for it*, but not expect it or demand it.

Think of student loan forgiveness. It's called "forgiveness" for a reason, and no political leader to date has chosen to forgive us those debts. I would love to have my compounding-interest student loan debt forgiven. But does the Department of Education have to? Must they? No. Would it be nice for them to? Very. Do I want them to forgive *everyone's* student debt? Yes, today. But as much as I hate it, as much as I want control over it, that choice is theirs to make— by virtue of our political leadership.

Forgive if you want, if it brings you joy, if it leads you toward love, if it is part of your peace. Forgiveness is a beautiful gift. But don't let societal, religious, or other pressures drive you to forgive if that act costs you your peace, health, safety, or heart.

UNDERSTAND TRAUMA

When I first left, I'd wake up in the middle of the night looking for him, only to remember that he was gone. Or rather, that I'd left. This is important because trauma has an extraordinary impact on our brains.

Dr. Peter Levine writes in his book *Trauma and Memory*:

> For well over a century we have understood that the imprints of trauma are stored not as narratives about bad things that happened sometime in the past, but as physical sensations that are experienced as immediate life threats—right now. In the intervening time we have gradually come to understand that the difference between ordinary memories (stories that change and that fade with time) and traumatic memories (recurring sensations and movements that are accompanied by intense negative emotions of fear, shame, rage, and collapse) is the result of a breakdown of the brain systems that are responsible for creating "autobiographical memories." . . . Traumatized people get stuck in the past: They become obsessed with the horror they consciously want to leave behind, but they keep behaving and feeling as if it is still going on. Unable to put the trauma behind them, their energy is absorbed by keeping their emotions under control at the expense of paying attention to the demands of the present. By safely replaying the old events in their minds and then constructing an imaginary satisfactory conclusion—something they had been unable to do during the original event because they had been too overwhelmed by helplessness and horror—they could begin to fully realize that they had, in fact, survived the trauma and could resume their lives. [4]

I used to think there was no value in the memories, in the waking up at night, confused about where I lived and who I was with. It was frightening, confusing, and annoying. The majority of the terror happened in the first waking moments, when my eyes shot open, and I couldn't identify the room shadows in the darkness. *Why is that window there? Whose comforter am I under? Where is my husband? Oh, this is the room I rent. My husband is gone.*

But then I started to work within the fear.

When I'd wake up confused, instead of pushing my mind for answers, I'd let it race. I'd allow it to go through the thoughts and feelings of the moment without trying to gain solid footing. I would simply lie there and just be—focusing on recognizing my own safety as opposed to making sense of the moment. After a while, I was less confused, though still sad. But it was the confusion that caused my distress, not necessarily the sadness.

Trauma, as many have written, shows up in the body. Physically, cognitively (i.e., confusion, irritation, dexterity, balance issues), emotionally, and more. Returning to the work of Bessel van der Kolk, in an interview with psychotherapist David Bullard for Psychotherapy.net he said,

> Trauma is much more than a story about the past that explains why people are frightened, angry or out of control. Trauma is re-experienced in the present, not as a story, but as profoundly disturbing physical sensations and emotions that may not be consciously associated with memories of past trauma. Terror, rage and helplessness are manifested as bodily reactions, like a pounding heart, nausea, gut-wrenching sensations and characteristic body movements that signify collapse, rigidity or rage. . . . The challenge in recovering from trauma is to learn to tolerate feeling what you feel and knowing what you know without becoming overwhelmed. There are many ways to achieve this, but all involve establishing a sense of safety and the regulation of physiological arousal.[5]

Understanding my trauma, and learning how to navigate it, was directly tied to feeling safe. I feel most safe in my own home, specifically in my own bed. I encourage you to find a safe place—not an internet-declared "safe space"—but a place that you genuinely feel safe in, and dock yourself there when the trauma feels too weighty.

◯

Moving past the initial shock of leaving and starting down the pathway of healing is going to take a lot longer than you know.

The worst advice I've ever received was from a family member in response to the death of a close friend. They said: "You've got to just get up and move on. They're not coming back so you gotta get on with your life." This was less than a week after that friend had passed away suddenly.

Getting up and moving on is possible, even critical. But it has to come in its own time, at the pace you decide. Healing is beautiful, continuous, sensitive, and intimate. And I hope you begin to see healing as sustained freedom. Because I view everything, and I do mean everything, through the lens of *liberation*.

In the anthology *Women on Divorce*, Ann Patchett writes:

> In time, a lot of time, after I left Friday's and got a fellowship that allowed me to write my first novel, I came to see that there was something liberating about failure and humiliation. Life as I had known it had been destroyed so completely, so publicly that in a way I was free, like I imagine anyone who walks away from a crash is free. I didn't have expectations anymore, and no one seemed to expect anything from me. I believed that nothing short of a speeding car could kill me. I knew there was nothing I couldn't give up. Even writing, which was my joy and greatest source of self-definition, I could give up if I had to. Divorce is in the machine now, like love and birth and death. Its possibility informs us, even when it goes untouched. And if we fail at marriage, we are lucky we don't have to fail with the force of our whole life. Sometimes I dream of an eighth sacrament, the sacrament of divorce. Like communion, it is a slim white wafer on the tongue. Like confession, it is forgiveness. Forgiveness is important, not so much for what we've done wrong, but for what we feel we need to be forgiven for. Family, friends, God, whoever loves us, forgives us, takes us in again. They are thrilled by our life, our possibilities, our second chances. They weep with gladness that we did not have to die.[6]

Leaving that relationship gave me my life back. In my abusive marriage, I essentially felt I had given up my existence, lost the essence of who I am. Choosing to divorce gave me a permission slip to pursue life again. In both leaving and in my healing process, I didn't feel like I lost anything; I felt like I won. And I hope, in your continuous healing process, you feel like you've won too.

Chapter 10

GOOD LOVE

"To be loved is to feel more capable, to be able to exceed whatever you think possible."
—Ashon Crawley

This was my favorite chapter to write.

Some folks say, "You only need to love yourself!" I think that's absurd. I say, I only need to love whoever I want. And when I choose who I want to love, I want a good love.

I am so positive, so desperately optimistic about the possibility of experiencing a healthy relationship. I believe intensely in the transformative power of love, in its possibilities, and its promises. And I've been close; my second husband loved me and treated me very well. But now, I am excited for a beautiful love that *sticks*.

Good love is fun. Not all the time, but most. Good love gives you space to protect your emotional boundaries. Good love offers mutual recognition, a *seeing* that acknowledges and embraces who you truly are.

I want a good love; I am a good love. I see love in all parts of my life. When my nephews jump in my arms, I see love. When my brother smiles at me, I see love. When someone kisses my back or neck while holding me close, I see love. Love is an abiding part of my life, and romantically, I yearn for it.

I've tried a lot of love, and many have tried to love me. But my new dedication to walking away from what feels wrong has helped protect my heart, and I constantly thank myself for committing to that. I cannot love everyone I date, and not everyone can love me, and that's okay. What I call my *"cost of loving,"* that is, the amount of love needed to cover my basic emotional needs, such as trust, security, affection, and prioritization, is high. Figuring out who I can, and cannot love, is the challenge.

So, let's talk about love.

WHY LOVE?

I enjoy reading old, yellow-hued, dusty sociological or psychological books.

For one, I find them entertaining in that they largely ignored the existence of women in speech ("he," "him," "his"), as if women's needs and desires were not suitable for appreciative study, only scientific study.

But there is one book I always circle back to. I bought two print copies years ago in case I loan one out. It's called *The Art of Loving* by Erich Fromm. One of the more famous quotes from his book is, "Love is the only sane and satisfactory answer to the problem of human existence."

But there is a section at the beginning of the book that speaks to why we need love.

> This attitude—that nothing is easier than love—has continued to be the prevalent idea about love despite the overwhelming evidence to the contrary. There is hardly any activity, any enterprise, which is started with such tremendous hopes and expectations, and yet, which fails so regularly, as love. If this were the case with any other activity, people would be eager to know the reasons for the failure and to learn how one could do better—or

they would give up the activity. Since the latter is impossible in the case of love, there seems to be only one adequate way to overcome the failure of love—to examine the reason for this failure, and to proceed to study the meaning of love. The first step to take is to become aware that love is an art, just as living is an art; if we want to learn how to love, we must proceed in the same way we have to proceed if we want to learn any other art, say music, painting, carpentry, or the art of medicine or engineering. Envy, jealousy, ambition, any kind of greed are passions; love is an action, the practice of human power, which can be practiced only in freedom and never as a result of compulsion. Love is an activity, not a passive affect; it is a "standing in," not a "falling for."[1]

I'm enchanted by the idea that love is an art. When I visit museums, particularly fine art museums, I discover so many pieces that have been created by artists far and near, very few of which I fully understand. Abstract art, which I find interesting but not necessarily delightful, is so subjective that it can be hard to find any common ground or way to relate.

But love? *Mmmm.* Love is that human activity with the power to imagine, create, fulfill, confuse, endure, and sustain. Love is art, and as Fromm says, a "practice of human power." I want to tell you about the kinds of love that are important as you move through reinvention and healing.

SURE LOVE

I once dated a guy for two months, and in those two months, he fell hard. After just a few weeks, he'd bought me a pair of Jordans, scheduled three trips to visit me in Chicago, and asked me to meet his mother. I had begun to fall, but not as quickly or deeply as he did, so all of this was very overwhelming. Shortly before the ending, I started having nightmares about H. And that was jarring, because my frequent nightmares about him had quieted. It seemed that I was happy-ish while conscious and haunted while sleeping.

There were a few things I didn't like about the relationship—how he could never be wrong, how his wrongness would become attributable to something that I did, his argumentativeness disguised as a desire for debate. But he treated me nicely, bought me things, frequently visited since he lived out of town. Still, at night, H. kept appearing in my dreams.

Soon I began to connect my evening nightmares to that relationship. While not abusive, certain things that partner did reminded me of H. And I ignored that mental note because, again, he treated me nicely. But my gut, or as my grandma would call it, my "spirit," would not let me move on.

I decided to have a conversation with him about my feelings.

"I think the nightmares are connected to you," I said.

"What does that mean?" he asked, genuinely confused.

"You know how I always say I don't like arguing with you, and you can never apologize for anything? That's how my H. was."

"Nah," he replied sharply. "I am not abusive, Beverly. Don't put that on me."

"No, I'm not saying you are," I said. "But I need a break from this to figure out what's going on with me."

He was silent on the phone. My intention going into this conversation was to minimize the emotional impact of being compared to H., but the silence let me know I was unsuccessful in that.

"Love is supposed to be unconditional," he said, finally speaking. "You breaking up with me? Over my personality? Come on, Bev, that's not fair."

"But it's how I feel," I replied, not backing down. "This relationship is not good for me. If that's conditional, so be it."

We went back and forth for another few minutes, him demanding a longer explanation to the end of our sixty-day relationship until, finally, I said I'd have to go. And I did go; I hung up the phone and walked away from it. When I got back to the phone, there were missed calls and an email. I chose not to call him back or respond to the email.

For the record, I am okay with conditional love. I tried unconditional love in the first marriage, and well, here is this book.

Love, sometimes, has endings. One thing I was sure of was that that love, with that man, was not for me.

Over the next few months, he proved me correct by digitally dragging me, initially nonstop but then a bit more infrequently, on Twitter. He complained about me ghosting him—which is impossible to do if you have a breakup conversation as we had. His actual complaint was that I no longer spoke with him; he believed he was entitled to sustained post-breakup contact with me.

He sent emails asking for clarification or more conversation, accused me of cheating on him, asked if he could come to visit to talk, but I had no more to say; I was working through it all myself. We shared many internet friends who knew we'd broken up, so instead of being private, the breakup was playing out on Twitter. Well, his side of it was—not mine. I never tweeted to him or about him after our final talk.

Six months after the breakup, he sent me a closure email. Now, I don't think closure is necessarily always a good idea; sometimes, it can be another reason for staying in contact with someone we should let go of. But he decided to send a lengthy but clear message about how he felt. And, because time had provided me some clarity, this email I responded to.

From: Bev
Date: Thursday, December 6, 2012 at 10:59 a.m.
Subject: Re:
To: ▮▮▮▮

Hi,
Thanks for writing this email. I can see it was well thought-out, and that is appreciated.

I don't, however, think it was necessary to hit send. But you did, so let me clarify some things.

I didn't break up with you for any reason other than the fact that you weren't the one. I didn't fully understand it at the time, so I couldn't properly articulate what I was feeling. I apologize for that, because it is hard to accept a breakup when you don't know the full reason. I'm very sorry I couldn't explain it. I needed to reflect. But after all of these months I do understand why. The reason I was having dreams about my ex near the time that we ended was because you share a lot of similar personality traits. To be clear again, I'm not saying you are abusive. What I am saying is that our personalities would have come to blows sooner or later and I was not willing to stick around for that. Or work through it. You are strong willed and outspoken, which is good. But it can also be bad. The conflicts about admitting you are wrong, knowing everything . . . and my own conflicts about feeling that things were moving too fast in our relationship. These things matter. It would have been a shame for us to continue moving forward if I knew we wouldn't last. That wouldn't have been fair to you, especially. One thing I realize is that not every person is meant for each other, no matter how much love there is or how well they get along. There can be an awesome connection and crazy chemistry, but the intricacies matter.

I, too, had to unfollow people who follow you. Since July, I've seen RT'ed, snarky comments about your last #her, or your ex. Enough people know exactly who I was. And that is SO disrespectful. Yet another reason why I know us moving on was the right choice. You bleed on Twitter . . . you share almost everything. Intimate, personal details. And I'm a private person about many aspects of my private life. It's obvious that you need someone who is just as public as you or is willing to allow you to share intimate details of your relationship. That is not me.

I know these words are probably hard to digest. We just weren't meant to be.

I hope you find the one.

He responded angrily. I was proud however, because my spirit *had* given me warning signs about him, and when looking back, the love bombing—a term used to describe people who overwhelm their partners with affection and gifts—was also a warning sign, even with no violence. But the warnings my spirit gave me were useful in that they taught me to *trust myself*, listen to my thoughts, and believe my heart when it says, "this is wrong."

What I want to say about "sure love" is that it is okay to change your mind. If you are unsure, it is okay to take a breath, pause, and work through the uncertainties. If you are sure, it's okay to move forward. If you are sure that a love is not for you, it is okay to assert that with care and end it.

The good love that I want invites freedom to choose. On my parents' fortieth wedding anniversary, I asked them what the secret to staying together is. My dad said, "We just keep choosing each other, and we're sure about it."

I want to be chosen with surety, and if the day comes when I'm no longer the choice, I want to be let go with grace. I want to be sure, and I want a sure partner. My friend elle wrote an Instagram caption under a photo of them and their partner. It read, "Happy Anniversary! I'll love you for as long as you'll have me." And it still resonates as such a beautiful, healthy way to do love.

In *All about Love*, bell hooks writes about how loveless she felt in primary relationships and how she had to learn what love is and how to do it to change that. She argues that she engaged in love that was unclear and difficult. That knowledge is part of what I call our "love pattern"—the models, behaviors, and circumstances in which we have historically participated in love. She goes on to write that in relationships with men, she'd chosen to pursue ones who were wounded emotionally, not interested at all in being loving, but who wanted the feel of experiencing the love she had to give them. I relate to that—for a long time, my love pattern was trying to love people who were unsure about their love for me, people who were interested in taking love but not so much in expressing it. The men, in particular, had a pattern of coming over for the sex (that I happily gave them) but couldn't ask how my day was going or take me on a date. As bell hooks articulates, relationships based on affection and not any semblance of loving are more manageable; the risk that loving someone requires is not as high in these relationships.

I believe in the existence of micro-grief, that is, grieving the small(ish) losses in life, like a missed job opportunity or canceling a planned vacation for unforeseen reasons. This applies to love and dating as well. Even today, still, I don't like what's called the "talking stage," because it could lead to the development of entry-level romantic feelings. And if it doesn't work out, well now you have another person to grieve. And there's no medicine for grief—no prescription to take to the pharmacy. You just have to go through it. And I don't want another person to grieve.

When a romance fails early and then you hop back on The (Dating) Apps to meet someone new and start another, then another, then another, it's like *a thousand little paper cuts* on the heart. Then, when love or something like it takes root, you must develop the emotional language to process when that love becomes unsustainable, like with ghosting or cushioning.

But I'm committed to approaching new people in an effort to find a sure love openly, confidently, and with care, without projecting past dangers onto them.

But having a sure love begins with having a *clear* love.

CLEAR LOVE

My longtime therapist asked me a series of questions in response to me feeling unprotected in the dating world.

"I overshare early," I said.

"Why?"

"I don't know. I feel like me sharing things about myself helps people open up and share things about themselves," I replied. "Sometimes it's one way—me sharing and them not sharing. And if it goes on like that for too long, then I start feeling uncomfortable."

"So, are you only sharing in hopes that it creates an environment for openness, or are you sharing because you want to share whatever it is you're sharing?" she asked. I thought for a minute.

"I think half-and-half. But the more I share, the deeper the sharing goes. And if the person I'm getting to know doesn't meet my sharing with their own sharing—even if it's something small—then I feel like I'm out there, open-hearted, all alone."

"Do you ask them to share? As in, directly saying, 'Tell me something about yourself?'" she asked.

"Most of the time, I do, but I also don't want to make anyone feel like they have to share. Like if sharing things is a personal boundary for them."

Her head tilted to the side.

"I think deep vulnerability at an early stage can be a boundary for some people. But, opening up to share *basic* things about yourself and your life is a natural part of getting to know someone new," she said. "And resistance to answering any questions at all is something to think carefully about."

I nodded.

"It sounds like," she continued, "you know that you tend to share, then share more and more if you're the only one sharing, believing that the key to unlocking someone else's door is to have your own door open. But how are you keeping yourself safe with the door to your heart standing wide open like that? Not everyone deserves your intimacy."

I thought for a minute.

"I don't know how to keep myself safe, really. Not emotionally."

"Let's start by setting some ground rules for sharing," she said. "Each time you start dating someone new, ask yourself: What do I *want* to share? What things are off-limits? What do I want to know from *them*?"

That evening, I made a list based on those three questions.

What do I want to share? I want to share the basics of my immediate family—our names, where we all live, and underscore our closeness—particularly the closeness I have with my brother. I want to share that I have three nephews and that I'm the godmother to the youngest one. And should anything happen to his parents, I'll be raising one (or three) boys. I want to share my passion for art and music; how I love poetry and tea-making. And I want to share my shortlist of wants and needs. For example, I need gentleness, stability, and for my partner to "show up." I want to share that every night at 9:30 p.m., my phone automatically goes on "Do Not Disturb," and you'll have to call twice in a row if it is an emergency.

What things are off-limits? My biological mother and siblings. That's a sensitive part of my life, and I'll only talk about them when

I'm ready. I also don't want to go into detail about my past reproductive health choices. I'll share that I froze my eggs and had a hysterectomy early, because that may impact whether someone wants a long-term future with me, but that's it. The many choices I made about my reproductive health before that are also very personal.

As you can see, though, my off-limits list is short. Once I feel comfortable and safe, I'm mostly an open book. But what do I want to know from them? What, at a base level, do I need to know to feel comfortable moving forward in dating?

I want to know, *what is your vision of partnership?* If there is one thing I know to be true, it's that almost every person you meet will have a different idea of partnership. Every coalition, board, and company create a shared vision and mission to guide their collective work. So, what does a relationship look like to you? What is your expectation regarding daily communication? Who is responsible for routine tasks? How do we resolve issues? Who walks the dog in the morning? (Because there will be dogs.) What do the holidays look like for you?

I want to know where you come from, who your people are. What influences and shapes you? Do you have kids, or are you expecting any currently? If so, what is your relationship with the other parent, if there is one? And yes, after the first few dates, I want to know your social media handles. (Gotta make sure you're not on the internet using terms like "gay agenda," "females," or "those feminists.") Gotta check all your images for red hats with white lettering, beginning in 2015.

Another area of creating a clear love is asking yourself, "Are they good for me *now*?" Earlier in the book, I mentioned how I'd carried a profound, long-suffering hope in others, even in the face of disappointment. I've had to learn how to separate *my hope* from the *current reality*. By asking ourselves, "Is this person good for me now?" we are consciously drawing a clear line between how good it *could be* and how good it *is*. Because "could be" is not "is." And "could be" might never manifest.

Survivors spend a lot of time hoping for the best, hoping for a different outcome, hoping for change. By looking at what *is*, what is right in front of us, we can make decisions based on our present needs. Grounding ourselves in the present while making room for hope—not making hope the *focal point*. There is space for hope; hope is good. But only if there is movement in accordance with that hope. Hope without action is fantasy.

SWEET LOVE

Tenderness—that is what I wanted when I was ready to explore love and affection after surviving abuse.

I needed tenderness. I wanted gentleness. I liked to be cared for emotionally and handled softly. I bet you would, too.

Stacia L. Brown, a producer at North Carolina Public Radio who I came across on Twitter back in 2013, is one of my favorite writers. What I find most wonderful about her is that she has kept a blog for nearly a decade, regularly updating readers about her life.

In 2015, she wrote a blog post titled "Happiness Happens." It begins:

> I like extravagant gifts: costly travel, pricey meals, good wine, undivided attention, genuine laughter at a joke I've made, forgiveness. I don't often get those things and when I do, typically, I give them to myself. This is, in part, because grown-ups told me, when I was small, that it's impolite to ask for gifts, immodest to carry myself as though I expect or deserve them, imprudent to confess aloud that I desire them.
>
> I come from a line of women unaccustomed to getting what we want, unaccustomed to granting ourselves permission to voice our desires. We have never known what could be asked for without the answer of a scold or denial, without the answer of silence or a promise unfulfilled. My grandmother, a middle child among ten siblings; my mother, the only child of a single teenage mother; me, born to my single mom when she was nineteen: We weren't offered much in the way of lavishness.

That history matters.

How painful it becomes to live lowlier than you ought, to cloak yourself in denial of need or of pleasure, to constantly settle for less than you'd like. Over time, it means forgetting what you like. It results in an uncertainty of what would truly make you happy and, for a time, it seems that you are in a state of perpetual discontent. Nothing is ever quite as pleasant as you'd want it to be.

There are ways to end this. Each one begins with opening your mouth, with saying: I want. and allowing it to be both public and true. Let it breathe I want. and animate I want. and demand undivided attention. Happiness happens at the intersection of courage and confession, risk and recollection. I am never prouder of myself than when I choose to stand at those crossroads. [2]

Let me tell you why I love these words and what any of them has to do with sweet love.

Often, when showing Black women under the lens of passion or care, we are one of two things: a tool to be used as a sexual outlet by others, having no absolute autonomy—physically present but voiceless—or someone who is entirely void of desire or sensuality at all, figuratively neutered and present only to serve in some other way, for instance, caring for another's child or cooking. We have no needs and no wants—no opinions on being loved or how to care for us. But here, in this passage, Stacia opens with a list of the luxurious items she enjoys and how she is to be *made happy*. I hope that all of us discover and can express the sweet things we want in this life.

As I moved through surviving, reinventing, and desiring, I needed to explore my relationship to pleasure.

Before that exploration, pleasure was tied to shame. I was raised steeped in the Christian religious tradition where self-sacrifice was deemed crucial and above all else. You live to serve and be of service to all. And that sacrifice was both tangible and intangible— the sacrifice of money, time, needs, enjoyment, and rest. Pleasure, the pursuit of it and its receipt, was largely negative; it was a signal of indulgence and, therefore, sin. Even down to what I ate and how much I ate, pleasure was to be restricted and controlled, not pursued or understood as a healthy part of a balanced life. This concept was so deep in my psyche that in 2007, I self-published a book about the shame of "sexual sin" and my hope for redemption. Since then, I've had to reprogram my heart, body, and intentions to receive pleasure with joy and to *seek it* courageously.

While I value both service *and* sacrifice, I've seen the emotional state in which service to others and never to yourself can leave you.

My parents lived this principle through near-constant sacrifice, even to complete strangers. The goal, to be like Jesus, who, in that faith tradition, offered the most significant sacrifice—his life. I did not know much about self-care or even self-compassion: sacrifice, sacrifice, sacrifice. Give, give, give.

I lived the same self-sacrificial life as my family for many years until it broke me. I was so exhausted, so empty, that I retreated inward, rejecting relationships with others in fear that those relationships would require relentless surrender.

I remember dating a youth pastor once, and he'd invited me to an evening church service to hear a celebrity pastor preach. We had been to several services already that week, and I was tired, out of money to put in the offering basket, and annoyed because I did not even like the people in that church. They were cold and demanding, judgmental under the guise of "care" for my soul.

"I can't make it tonight," I said after he called to confirm I was going.

"Why not? What you got going on tonight?"

"Nothing, I just don't feel like going."

I could hear his confusion within the silence on the other end of the phone.

"I mean, I don't always feel like going, but when it's like that, you just gotta push through. There's a blessing in store."

I like blessings, but I also like rest. Even today, I'll choose rest over everything else.

Realizing I was not going to get him to understand why I was choosing rest over whatever blessing would be there waiting in the church sanctuary that night, I kindly told him goodbye and hung up the phone.

Now, what does any of this have to do with sweet love?

The sweet, tender love I want also includes me giving that sweetness to myself. Intuiting my needs and honoring them, however those needs present themselves. Sacrificing, yes, but in the way that those sacrifices make *comfortable*. Sacrificing quiet time to visit my nephews and stay up late, laughing loudly and playing video games. Sacrificing money that I'd like to spend on a new travel coffee mug to give cash to someone at an intersection. Sacrificing takeout for myself one evening so that I can have money to treat a friend to dinner. The sacrifices I make now are *balanced and thoughtful*; I no longer do it out of the pursuit of righteousness, but out of genuine love for others, based on the love I feel deeply for myself.

But yes, it also applies to everyone else. And as Stacia L. Brown writes, we must feel brave enough to ask for the kind of sweetness that we want. In the same blog, Stacia L. Brown writes about a company that offered to send her a gift. She saw that she wanted two gifts when presented with the options, though just one had been offered to her. So, she asked for both.

> In all confession, there resides an element of risk. Courting rejection in exchange for a chance at delight: this is the writer's only real ambition. This risk is nearly a friend, a long-familiar.
>
> So . . . I said yes, though I apologized for what may be viewed as greed: I wanted both the strawberries and the cheesecake trio. I said yes, with a slight blush and a bitten lip, as I always associate gifts like these with the lovers I wish I had asked for them. In turn, the company waved its magic wand. Three days later, the package arrived: one dozen chocolate covered strawberries and a lovely assortment of miniature cheesecakes.

What I want, more than almost anything, is for us to say yes to sweetness. Yes, to the things that will make us happy. Yes, to the gifts we want, and yes to the people we want.

In the introduction to this book, I wrote that I hope love brings sweetness to you. I wrote that because I want it for me, too. I have not known a sweet, lasting love. It's always sweet in the beginning when the stakes seem high. But I want love to be sweet in mundane moments; I want the stakes of keeping my heart always to be high.

GIVING LOVE

"Your love is thick," a lover of mine once said. "It's heavy, like a blanket. Sometimes it gets hot when you are under there, but other times, it's comfortable."

She was not wrong, that lover. In fact, I used to call myself an *over lover*, but I've pulled back on that a bit. In truth, I am an "all-in" lover; I love completely. The thing is, I love to love. A guy I had a brief fling with called me a "little lovebug."

It is because I have always felt fully myself when I give love, like God, the stars, the wind, and the chaos of thunder all joined together and spun me into a person who emits love like perfume, the scent of which can be smelled by anyone who passes by. My friends would tell you that I love love; I carry a little love in my purse like Beyoncé's hot sauce, just in case I run into someone who needs a bit. I put a tremendous amount of importance on loving my friends, regardless of gender identity. Early on, after my second marriage ended, I decided to focus on the kind of life that I wanted, and I wanted a life filled with love. And it's okay to make love a focus so long as that focus stays in balance with other areas of your life, like general health or personal goals. And so, my focus became loving whoever was in my life fully. And my friends were in my life.

The *Five Love Languages* is a popular book by Gary Chapman. If you're familiar with it, you know that he lists five general ways people experience love—by expressing or needing these specific types of love. The five love languages, according to Chapman, are words of affirmation, quality time, physical touch, acts of service, and receiving gifts.[3]

I've taken the quiz that tells what your love languages are a few times, and each time I received different results; sometimes, my number one love language is physical touch, which is ironic and poignant, given my now altered relationship with touch; other times, it's quality time. Personally, I'm a huge fan of acts of service; I hate taking out the garbage.

But when it comes to giving love, I use my understanding of *my own* love languages to decide what kind of love I am capable of giving to others, friends, family, or romantic partners. This might seem to be in reverse, as love languages are designed to inform our intentions on what sort of love to receive. And it's imperative to find out what someone's love language is if they believe in this theory. But I find understanding my love languages so valuable for providing clear direction in the area of giving love.

My last quiz gave me three results, in this order: quality time, acts of service, and receiving gifts. Although I do give myself gifts every now and then, this is not about me. Knowing that one of my love languages is receiving gifts, I can redirect one of those gifts I'm planning to give myself toward someone else. If I love receiving gifts, why wouldn't someone else? Of course, some may not like gifts at all, and that's up to you to find out or perceive. But I've yet to give a thoughtful, loving gift to a loved one that they outright reject due to that not being their love language. My point is, as someone who likes gifts, I redirect the type of love I want to *receive* to someone I want to *give* love to.

For me, in terms of quality time, that means spending time together where there are no established plans. So not a "date night," just a casual chill night—once a week at minimum. It means taking trips together, every other month or so. And if I'm hoping to receive a love where we spend time together, I've decided to give that sort of love to others.

The year 2020 was a challenging year for a lot of reasons. For me, as a single person living alone, I ached for affection. After quarantine and vaccination, I tiptoed back out into the world with the sole purpose of spending quality time with my loved ones. I surprised my brother by showing up at his house one Saturday afternoon, clear across the country. I visited Washington, D.C., and bear-hugged two dear friends. No one was coming to see *me* because my love language is quality time; I made it a point to give the love of quality time to *others*. And in turn, I loved myself by also receiving that time.

Giving love is about understanding your capabilities and the boundaries of others and making space for a new life filled with love. Good love, to me, is gentle, sweet, sure, and clear. My grandma used to say, "giving good love never hurt nobody." *Good love* doesn't hurt anybody. It is conditional and rooted in the dignity of safety and respect for my wellbeing, boundaries, and life. And after what we survivors have lived through, we need the good love that giving love brings.

Ultimately, the good love that you want is solely up to you to define. As you begin to design your new life, ask yourself what good love feels like to you.

Chapter 11

UNSTUCK

"I hope the exit is joyful. And I hope never to return."
—Frida Kahlo

I've heard it said that all you have to do is get out of the abusive relationship and the rest will be easy. My experience is that the rest is hard. Not only hard, but confusing and heartbreaking. I didn't begin to feel a slight sense of normal until years after leaving; my emotions fluctuated between chaotic and dull. Surviving abuse, to be frank, is only the beginning. In this book, I've tried to express how beautiful life has become after surviving the abuse, but I hope that I've also been clear that it was an uphill climb. Rebuilding was a long process of beauty, making mistakes, disappointment, joy, confusion, clarity, and recovery.

That said, I think it's important not to deny that you're in pain over the end of a relationship. Breakups are already challenging; and a breakup from an abusive relationship is no different, except you have the added anguish of figuring out how to move on from what just happened to you.

The first thing I did, after settling into my new routine, was try to understand why the abuse happened in the first place. In staying with H., I made it part of my mission to figure out why he was abusive while still experiencing abuse. It may not seem like it based on part I of this book, but much of my marriage was stable. We had a lot of fun together; we enjoyed each other. From the songwriting to the road trips, adopting dogs and sitting on the beach, moving across the country together and planning a long life as a couple, we were in love. So, whenever the physical or emotional abuse showed up, I was puzzled by it.

After I left, I still had that same curiosity, just now in the safety of space. I went to the library and checked out a few of the more common domestic violence books at the time. The first one I read through was Lundy Bancroft's book, *Why Does He Do That?* While Bancroft focuses specifically on men who abuse, I liked this passage:

> I came to realize, through my experience with over two thousand abusers, that the abusive man wants to be a mystery. To get away with his behavior and to avoid having to face his problem, he needs to convince everyone around him—and himself—that his behavior makes no sense. He needs his partner to focus on everything except the real causes of his behavior. To see the abuser as he really is, it is necessary to strip away layer after layer of confusion, mixed messages, and deception. Like anyone with a serious problem, abusers work hard to keep their true selves hidden. Part of how the abuser escapes confronting himself is by convincing you that you are the cause of his behavior, or that you at least share the blame. But abuse is not a product of bad relationship dynamics, and you cannot make things better by changing your own behavior or by attempting to manage your partner better. Abuse is a problem that lies entirely within the abuser. [1]

I've maintained that the only person responsible for abuse is the one who committed it, and I understood that deeply. But it didn't quite answer the question of *why* for me. But there was a paragraph in James Gilligan's book *Preventing Violence* that did stick with me. It reads:

> The basic psychological motive, or cause, of violent behavior is the wish to ward off or eliminate the feeling of shame and humiliation—a feeling that is painful, and can even be intolerable and overwhelming—and replace it with its opposite, the feeling of pride. . . . The degree to which a person experiences feelings of shame depends on two variables: the way other people are treating him (with admiration and respect, or with contempt and disdain), and the degree to which he himself already feels proud or ashamed.[2]

That could be it in some cases, and I do believe much of abuse is tied to ego. Though I don't believe that the single cause of violence is shame, I understand what Dr. Gilligan is voicing. I believe that causes of violence other than shame are simply a desire to harm and control, a need to win. To have power over someone who loves or cares for you in an effort to keep them and that care close, to prevent it from walking away.

I recognize that there are factors other than choice that encourage violence. Poverty brought on by systemic racism and discrimination, intentional disparities in income and wealth, inequality, unemployment, socioeconomic vulnerability, how we are taught to express anger, or how we are taught to perform masculinity. Or, none of those could apply to my marriage and it could be that H. simply chose violence. I like to leave room for "none of the above" because life is unruly and does not always fit into boxes. But my point is, there are so many potential answers to "why?"

So, after a few months of trying to understand him, in an effort to understand our entire relationship, I decided to stop. I no longer want to understand; I'm not on that quest anymore. I support those survivors, academics, activists, and changemakers who have made understanding abusers part of their work. But I wanted to move on from it and moving on meant letting go.

Perhaps the most difficult part of he and I ending our marriage was letting go.

Letting go of the dreams we'd made, letting go of the hope that things would one day be like they were in the beginning of our relationship, letting go of the consistent intimacy that comes from being in an established partnership, letting go of the cute apartment we shared.

Letting go of the long, snuggly hugs from him that I'd never get again, letting go of his kisses. Letting go of the very specific-to-us goals we'd established as partners, like composing an entire film score together, or building a studio in a house we'd buy so that we could have friends and other artists come make music with us. Letting go of it all.

Letting go is hard, and I wish I'd heard that more once I left. Writer Jamie Anderson wrote, "Grief, I've learned, is really just love. It's all the love you want to give but cannot. All that unspent love gathers up in the corners of your eyes, the lump in your throat, and in that hollow part of your chest. Grief is just love with no place to go."[3]

And it is, straight like that. I loved my ex-husband, but I chose myself. I chose to protect, secure, and build myself, without that love. So where did it go? Well, at first, nowhere. It was love turned sadness, turned emptiness. But after a while, I'd say about two or three years had passed since I left him, I finally decided to capture that wandering, targetless love and aim it at myself.

But not in a played out "love yourself and you will be better!" way. Because I've always loved myself and being in an abusive relationship didn't change that. I loved myself before it, during it, and after it.

I credit my grandmother, Ella Mae, with teaching me self-love. She was a quiet but certain woman, born in 1916 and raised by her sister—why, I'm not sure. What I am sure of, though, is that she believed in herself and in her ability to do anything she wanted. And that "she wanted" is doing a lot of work here; my grandma did not try to do everything. She did what she wanted. When she wanted a rose garden, she got on her hands and knees and dug holes at the side of her house and planted roses. Speaking of houses, when she wanted a house, she asked my grandpa to build her one. Speaking of my grandpa, when she wanted to marry him, she did; he had to ask her more than once.

It's that *want* my grandma taught me that was the key to self-love. Some would say "go out there and do this or that!" In fact, I've done that several times in this book. But I learned from her that if the this-es or thats weren't things I wanted to do, then I was not honoring the part of myself that sought the pleasure of making me happy, first.

Honor your wants.

My grandma taught me to center myself while making room for *others*, especially those you love. And we can do both—we can make ourselves a priority while also inviting others into whatever space feels comfortable for them in our lives.

Through her work and life, Frida Kahlo taught me public self-love and turning pain to beauty. Pointing her self-perception outward, she yearned to make beauty of it, not just in art but in relation to others. She once said,

> I used to think I was the strangest person in the world but then I thought there are so many people in the world, there must be someone just like me who feels bizarre and flawed in the same ways I do. I would imagine her and imagine that she must be out there thinking of me too. Well, I hope that if you are out there and read this and know that, yes, it's true I'm here, and I'm just as strange as you.[4]

In painting herself repeatedly, Kahlo reminds me to pay attention—to my eyes, to my lips, to my cheeks. To all the things that make me, me.

Janet Jackson taught me sensual, tantric love. The kind that speaks your desires out loud with *no shame*.

Toni Cade Bambara taught me love through self-revolution. Love through taking care to move cautiously and deliberately with your own life. In her anthology, *The Black Woman*, Bambara writes,

> Revolution begins with the self, in the self. The individual, the basic revolutionary unit, must be purged of poison and lies that assault the ego and threaten the heart. . . . It may be lonely. Certainly painful. It'll take time. We've got time. That of course

is an unpopular utterance these days. Instant coffee is the hall-
mark of current rhetoric. But we do have time. We'd better take
the time to fashion revolutionary selves, revolutionary lives, revolutionary relationships.[5]

So, during my marriage when tensions were bad, I could still look at
myself in the mirror with love. I didn't always like what I saw, but I
loved her. Because I knew that in the end, I'd find myself circling
back to the devotion that precedes self-love, chasing my own joy.

The romantic love I'd reserved for *him*? That is what I had to
arrest.

One task of the memoirist is to tell stories from their life experiences. I would be wrong, I think, to not name the discomfort I felt in
writing some of this book—to reveal the actions of H. that were
both painful and life-changing for me. But, recognizing that he is
human, and in me writing these memories, his life may also change.

I have a responsibility to survivors, and part of that responsibility
for me has been to share my own story, to, as I wrote earlier in this
book, be open to being seen. I wrote about the ways his life interacted with mine during those years. Where I've struggled then is in
writing about my ex-husband as part of my story, knowing that the
most painful parts for me may also be painful parts for him—parts
that he thought would remain between us. I've tried to handle this
with the care that it deserves, knowing that my words are true, but
recognizing that he has a life to live.

So, I sit with that as any writer-survivor would. Wondering
where the healthy boundaries are and thinking through how I can
express care now that this story is public.

I don't carry any anger toward H. In fact, I have love for him,
though I'm not in love with him or in touch with him. I've been
intentional about not naming him; publicly identifying him is not
something I regard as necessary for my healing. And I don't view
that as protecting him, but more so protecting myself. If I speak his
name to the public, then I have to see that name every time my story
is written about. And that isn't something I want to see, regardless
of frequency or context.

Even so, I do have empathy for him, though this empathy does not push me to reconnect. I don't think I'll ever know why he was abusive toward me; I don't know that he himself knows. But I have a deep compassion for the pain and, probably, the shame he carries knowing this was a part of him. That doesn't lead me to forgive the abuse, but it does provide resolution. I resolve that period of my life by saying: "I do not know." The beauty, for me, is in accepting that.

And you know how some people say: "I wouldn't trade [bad experience] for the world because it made me who I am today?" I do not feel that way. I would trade that experience if I could get back the incredibly vibrant, somewhat naïve, and amazingly optimistic young woman that I was before I met him. Every step I've taken since surviving abuse has been on a journey to recover parts of her again, blending her with the person I am today. And when storms come, I pray that they pass quickly. I've learned not to pray that storms don't come, because that isn't realistic. But the thing about storms is that they move; most will not just hover over one single spot. So when they come, I pray that they are fast-moving with no devastation.

It took what seemed like forever to leave the boarding house and that first temp job, but I moved out and kept going forward. I grew and changed, flexed new muscles, took some chances. Lost, won. Made new friends, moved on from some.

I got better jobs with more pay. I started writing again, though not in journals, but writing, nonetheless. Because I told you that healing is forever—I make that part of my life. I read Psalm 27:13 out loud every day, and I believe it. I attend biweekly therapy sessions. I institute a "Bev Day," one day of the week where I don't do *anything* that I don't want to do, even if that means the dishes pile up in the sink. I wear soft pants and tees, or long robes with no bra on. I sleep in on weekends, shamelessly. I love numerology and Lenormand Cards. I think psychics are cool.

I invest in myself in ways that remind me that I am free. If I can afford it, I'll take an unplanned road trip and stay in a nice hotel for a weekend. There is no one to stop me from buying however many strawberry kolaches I want. I read for pleasure, sitting in a beach chair by the ocean. I drink teas that I blend using herbs mostly from my own herb garden that correspond with how I feel that day. For anxiety, mix lavender, chamomile, and rosehip. For energy, rosemary and damiana. If I've got a chest cold, peppermint, elderberry, and hibiscus, with honey. For nausea, use ginger, lemon, and mint. For good mornings, a nice black tea with a little sugar, plus half and half.

I bought my first home in 2019, a small, one-story brick house with big windows in a more rural part of Texas. The community is surrounded by several farms, and there is a cow named Gertrude who frequently roams the area—not far from her herd though. And while I know that I won't always live next to her, I have a next-door neighbor, a Jamaican woman, who has become one of my dear friends. We share herbs from our gardens, look out for the other's package deliveries if one of us is out of town. When I had my hysterectomy, she cooked Jamaican food for me. During the COVID-19 pandemic, we each stood in our driveways yelling across to each other, smiling. She said, "Come outside every now and then so I know you're okay." She left a bottle of 70 percent Isopropyl Alcohol at my doorstep during the early stages of the pandemic when none was available. I still don't know how she found that bottle. We have a monthly wine date on her patio.

I've created a home for myself that feels like me and makes me feel soothed from the minute I walk in the door. I've decorated my home in ways that I like—jewel tones in the bedroom, dark neutrals in my office, light neutrals and pastels in the living room, white chairs in the dining room. I like it neat, and I keep things in their place because that helps ease my mind. I have a lot of art covering my walls, including a painting of an astronaut. It reminds me that not even the sky is the limit.

My favorite color is gold so there are gold accents everywhere—gold side tables, a gold stapler, a gold mug. Something I tried recently that I never expected is painting—mostly watercolors. It is something that reminds me to keep learning and growing and trying. I change my hairstyle every other week. I wear my nails long, painted red, because it makes me feel pretty. If I feel like roller-skating or scooter-riding at some random place, I'll go. It's a reminder to me: There's nothing stopping you. The doors to everything are *open*.

I use social media differently now, too. While I love that anonymity allows people to speak and connect without fear of discovery, one of my personal rules is not to debate—especially a contentious debate—with anyone who presents as anonymous. Because it's not a fair fight; I'm baring my whole self, and as a woman, risking my own safety, while whoever is attempting to argue me down gets to say whatever they want, then fade into obscurity without the threat of exposure or the challenge of accountability. I'm not signing up for that exchange. Either we're both accountable for what we put out into the world, or I don't engage.

I am intentional about the spaces I'm in, and when I'm in them. If you don't notice me in heavy or difficult places often, it's because I'm constantly seeking lightness . . . chasing after peace. I put a lot of thought into where I go and what engagements I take on because I'm so committed to inner peace. And while we can't escape hard spaces, particularly as advocates, we can limit our exposure to them if we understand what causes soreness in our emotional tender spots.

Many of the references and quotes throughout this book have been largely gendered, and that is because of the limited amount of research, resources, and data available on LGBTQ+ relationship abuse. While my story is also a cisgender heteroromantic one, I hope that this book encourages those not in this type of relationship to write their own stories of surviving abuse, so that we can shower them with love, praise, safety, and support as they rebuild and reimagine their own new lives.

To write this book, I've had to remember. That is, to place each limb in its originally birthed position, in the correct spot, so as not to disfigure the past. Then, I had to look at it plainly. I've written from a place of remembering, and when I couldn't remember, I did not write. And there were parts of my story too painful to reassemble, and I hope that has not left you wanting. If so, I'm sorry. If not, I'm glad.

When I started writing this book in 2015, the title was going to be "Unstuck," because I wanted to tell you how to get there. But the more I wrote, the more I realized I don't actually want to tell you how to get unstuck, because I want you to figure that out for yourself. It looks different for everyone, and I'm always skeptical of books that prescribe you an exact way to accomplish anything. Maybe you are someone with a disability. Maybe you experience transphobia. Maybe you are an immigrant who does not have full access in this country to the things that you deserve by virtue of your humanity. Maybe you experience racism or sexism in a different way than I do. Maybe there is deep poverty, a lack of family support, or priors that make it impossible to access certain services. Maybe you can't get help, particularly since therapy can be costly and inaccessible. Maybe you experience addiction or other health issues. You could be facing a million little things that I never had to face, or I may have faced things that you will not have to. So that alone gives us all a different path to becoming unstuck. It gives us all a different viewpoint on surviving.

But what binds us is our hope and our will. My longtime therapist always says that she admires my hope. In its purest form, my hope is what keeps me. And there's nothing else to add right there; I'm not going to say it keeps me going, because that wouldn't do my hope justice. My hope simply keeps me. At times, it keeps me in the place that I'm in, which is where I need to be. And at other times, my hope keeps me from pursuing things that I think I want that aren't in fact good for me. Most times my hope keeps me trying, you know? It just keeps me seeking.

What do I hope for, today? I hope for good finances. I hope for a full night's sleep, every night. I hope for better, because I know it's possible. I hope for opportunities to do creative work in television and film where I can bring stories to life. I hope to design a new superhero; I hope to produce romantic comedies and films about healthy love. If I must work for someone else, I hope that it is a thoughtful, progressive employer who values my gifts. I hope for love. I hope for orgasms. I hope that my three nephews will live the happiest, most successful life. I hope that I get to live closer to my brother one day. I hope that tomorrow I wake up to a beautiful sunrise with a full day that I've never seen ahead of me, fresh tea in hand. I hope to meet survivors. I hope we all have peace.

When you walk into my house, immediately to your right there is a large symbol on the wall called the Helm of Awe—made of runes from the runic alphabet, used in divination. The Helm of Awe itself is a symbol from Norse mythology—eight arms with spikes up and down, pointing in every direction, the stems meeting in the center, touching in the middle of a circle. It's considered to be one of the most powerful symbols of protection. In the center of the symbol on my wall is carved my name, Beverly Gooden, which gives the helm its meaning. Each time I walk out, I see a reminder that I am protected. When I walk in, it is there to say, *Welcome home to your safest place. A place that is yours, where there is no violence.*

In my bedroom there's a photo of a dragonfly. The coolest thing about dragonflies is that they can fly in every direction. They can move backward, forward, up or down, and sideways. Their very design is limitless. Dragonflies remind me that my path is not linear, that I must be agile, adaptable, and responsive.

Sometimes at night, I time travel. And I imagine that many people do—transport themselves to a different time and place in their lives. A happy moment, maybe a sad one. But me? I time travel to the future.

I travel to the soft beds of lovers I'll have, who may or may not stay, either is just fine. Maybe one, I'll marry. Maybe I'll choose to marry none. I travel to my nephews' graduations and other moments where our whole family will be present to love them and cheer them on.

Because I'm ambitious, I travel to stages and sofas where I'll speak to all of you about living—not just abuse. I want to make sure that is clear. This is not just about abuse. Or the past. Or who you were. Or what happened. It's about living. Because the real story of surviving abuse is about living again. About what to do with the burden of living, how to see the beauty in living, how to handle living. The possibilities of living, the struggles of living, the expectations of living. I serve as a witness to the future. I am not what you could be, I am what you *are*. I am here, present in this world, walking, head, and shoulders up, breathing in and out.

This story was about surviving, yes, but in my heart, I hope that you hear me telling you to live.

To keep going, to keep thinking, planning, wishing, and time traveling. To know that things change because that is the nature of living, which also means that this moment that you're in will change. If you're surviving abuse, I can't promise you that the moment you're in will change for the good in the immediate future, because it didn't for me (and also, no one can guarantee you that). But what I do know is that through the kindness of total strangers, through the Black spiritual tradition of relying on my ancestors to guide and protect me, through my family and friends, through prayer, through fighting, through tears, through trying, I survived.

And I'm living.

$\backsim$

National Domestic Abuse Helpline (UK)
0808 2000 247

List of UK Resources for Help and Support

Refuge – For women and children: www.refuge.org.uk
Refuge's National Domestic Abuse Helpline: 0808 2000 247
Galop – The LGBT+ anti-abuse charity: www.galop.org.uk/
National LGBT+ Domestic Abuse Helpline: 0800 999 5428 (run by Galop)
The Men's Advice Line – For male domestic abuse survivors: 0808 801 0327 (run by Respect)
Tender – Acting to end abuse: www.tender.org.uk
Sistah Space – Domestic abuse services for women of African-Caribbean heritage: www.sistahspace.org/
Southall Black Sisters – Support for the needs of Black (Asian and African-Caribbean) women: www.southallblacksisters.org.uk
Women's Aid – National charity working to end domestic abuse against women and children: https://www.womensaid.org.uk/

ACKNOWLEDGMENTS

Landon, Hudson, and Paxton, who saved my life.

Ella Mae, Terrence, Charlie, Yvonne, Kisha, and Debbie. All of my family in Ohio, Georgia, Alabama, Virginia, and West Virginia.

Larissa Melo Pienkowski, who I was drawn to from the moment we met. An encourager, editorial archer, and incredible agent; thank you for everything. I can't wait to see what's next on this journey.

Victoria Roddam and the Sheldon Press (Hodder & Stoughton) team: Thank you for believing in me.

Courtnie Ledet, MA, LPC, and Mary Kay Hamilton, LPC-S, Lori Kozlowski of More Light Media, Dr. Mary Elsbernd, Jill Grinberg Literary Management, Lissa Warren PR, Stephanie Nilva, Jessica Merrill, Theo Moll, and Keppler Speakers.

A. D. Smith, Kera Lawson, Geoff Blackman, Shyvon Lacy, Kyra Stephens, B. Monique Hutchinson, Antanique N. Adegbesokun, Brittany Jones, Kim Johnson, Marguerite Matthews, Miranda Gary, Julie Artieri, DaNella C. Knight, Megan Maddox, Quinn Hamilton, elle roberts, and J. Lavela.

NOTES

CHAPTER 1. STUCK

1. Jacob Goldstein, "How Sunk Cost Fallacy Applies to Love," *National Public Radio*, February 13, 2015, https://choice.npr.org/index.html?origin=https://www.npr.org/2015/02/13/385948508/how-sunk-cost-fallacy-applies-to-love.

2. Craig Malkin, "Why Do People Stay in Abusive Relationships?" *Psychology Today*, 2013, https://www.psychologytoday.com/us/blog/romance-redux/201303/why-do-people-stay-in-abusive-relationships.

CHAPTER 3. WHY WE STAY

1. Leslie Morgan Steiner, "Why Domestic Violence Victims Don't Leave," TED Talks, 2013, https://www.ted.com/talks/leslie_morgan_steiner_why_domestic_violence_victims_don_t_leave.

2. Beverly Gooden, "Why I Created the Why I Stayed (#WhyIStayed) Movement," *Beverly Gooden* (blog), September 8, 2014, https://www.beverlygooden.com/hear/whyistayed.

3. Robert F. Bornstein, "The Complex Relationship between Dependency and Domestic Violence: Converging Psychological Factors and So-

cial Forces," *American Psychologist* 61, no. 6 (September 2006): 595–606, https://doi.org/10.1037/0003-066x.61.6.595.

4. Lindsey Bever, "'Modern Family' Star Sarah Hyland Gets Restraining Order against Ex-Boyfriend," *Washington Post*, September 25, 2014, https://www.washingtonpost.com/news/morning-mix/wp/2014/09/25/modern-family-star-sarah-hyland-gets-restraining-order-against-ex-boy-friend/.

CHAPTER 4. NO ONE IS GOING TO SAVE YOU

1. Adrienne Adams, "Measuring the Effects of Domestic Violence on Women's Financial Well-Being," Center for Financial Security (CFS Research Brief), 2011, https://centerforfinancialsecurity.files.wordpress.com/2015/04/adams2011.pdf.

2. Morgan Brewton Johnson, "Once Again, Black Women Are Heroes. It's Time to Pay Up," *WBUR*, February 8, 2021, https://www.wbur.org/cognoscenti/2021/02/08/black-women-stacey-abrams-kamala-harris-morgan-brewton-johnson.

3. Urban Institute, "Structural Racism in America," September 21, 2016, https://www.urban.org/features/structural-racism-america.

4. Institute Staff, "11 Terms You Should Know to Better Understand Structural Racism," The Aspen Institute, August 29, 2017, https://www.aspeninstitute.org/blog-posts/structural-racism-definition/.

5. Elizabeth Chuck, "The U.S. Finally Has Better Maternal Mortality Data. Can It Now Help Save More Mothers?," *NBC News*, January 29, 2020, https://www.nbcnews.com/health/womens-health/u-s-finally-has-better-maternal-mortality-data-black-mothers-n1125896.

6. Amy Roeder, "America Is Failing Its Black Mothers," *Harvard Public Health Magazine*, December 21, 2018, https://www.hsph.harvard.edu/magazine/magazine_article/america-is-failing-its-black-mothers/.

7. Trymaine Lee, "How America's Vast Racial Wealth Gap Grew: By Plunder," *New York Times*, August 14, 2019, https://www.nytimes.com/interactive/2019/08/14/magazine/racial-wealth-gap.html.

8. Tulsa Historical Society and Museum, "1921 Tulsa Race Massacre," November 2018, https://www.tulsahistory.org/exhibit/1921-tulsa-race-massacre/.

9. Erin Logan, "A Florida Bank Refused to Cash an Elderly Black Woman's Check. Then They Called the Police on Her," *The Independent*, July 28, 2018, https://www.independent.co.uk/news/fargo-wells-bank-black-woman-cheque-florida-barbara-carroll-discrimination-a8467596.html.

10. Debra Kamin, "Black Homeowners Face Discrimination in Appraisals," *New York Times*, August 27, 2020, https://www.nytimes.com/2020/08/25/realestate/blacks-minorities-appraisals-discrimination.html.

11. Treva Lindsey, "The Urgent Crisis of Missing Black Women and Girls," Women's Media Center, February 20, 2020, https://womensmedia-center.com/news-features/the-urgent-crisis-of-missing-black-women-and-girls.

12. Matt Stieb, "What We Know about the Death of Black Lives Matter Activist Oluwatoyin Salau," *Intelligencer*, June 16, 2020, https://ny-mag.com/intelligencer/2020/06/what-we-know-about-the-death-of-acti-vist-oluwatoyin-salau.html.

13. Nada Hassanein, "Florida Protester Oluwatoyin Salau Killed in Tallahassee after Going Missing," *Tallahassee Democrat*, June 15, 2020, https://www.tallahassee.com/story/news/2020/06/15/oluwatoyin-salau-found-dead-tallahassee-black-lives-matter-protest-missing/3190021001/.

CHAPTER 5. A THEORY OF JUSTICE

1. Natalie J. Sokoloff and Ida Dupont, "Domestic Violence at the Intersections of Race, Class, and Gender," *Violence against Women* 11, no. 1 (January 2005): 42, https://doi.org/10.1177/1077801204271476.

2. Mikki Kendall, *Hood Feminism: Notes from the Women That a Movement Forgot* (New York: Penguin Books, 2021), 23.

3. Beth E. Richie, "A Black Feminist Reflection on the Antiviolence Movement," *Signs: Journal of Women in Culture and Society* 25, no. 4 (July 2000): 1137, https://doi.org/10.1086/495533.

4. Rebecca Miles-Doan, "Violence between Spouses and Intimates: Does Neighborhood Context Matter?" *Social Forces* 77, no. 2 (December 1998): 623, https://doi.org/10.2307/3005541.

5. J. Boudouris et al., "Behind Closed Doors: Violence in the American Family and Family Violence," *Contemporary Sociology* 11, no. 4 (July 1982), https://doi.org/10.1093/sw/26.4.353.

6. Michael D. Smith, "Sociodemographic Risk Factors in Wife Abuse: Results from a Survey of Toronto Women," *Canadian Journal of Sociology / Cahiers Canadiens de Sociologie* 15, no. 1 (1990): 39, https://doi.org/10.2307/3341172.

7. Robert J. Sampson and William Julius Wilson, "Toward a Theory of Race, Crime, and Urban Inequality," in *Crime and Inequality*, ed. John Hagan and Ruth D. Peterson (Stanford, CA: Stanford University Press, 1995), 44.

8. Ta-Nehisi Coates, "This Town Needs a Better Class of Racist," *The Atlantic*, May 1, 2014, https://www.theatlantic.com/politics/archive/2014/05/This-Town-Needs-A-Better-Class-Of-Racist/361443/.

9. adrienne maree brown, *Emergent Strategy: Shaping Change, Changing Worlds* (Chico, CA: AK Press, 2017), 10–11.

10. Mary Elsbernd and R. Bieringer, *When Love Is Not Enough: A Theo-Ethic of Justice* (Manila, Philippines: Ateneo De Manila University Press, 2008), 148.

11. Tanya Grant, "Domestic Violence Victims: An Examination of Advocates' Experiences and Impact on Services," *Journal of International Criminal Justice and Legal Issues* 1, no. 1 (2014): 31, https://digitalcommons.sacredheart.edu/cgi/viewcontent.cgi?article=1019&context=cj_fac.

12. Liz Kowalczyk, "Allegations of Employee Mistreatment Roil Renowned Brookline Trauma Center," *Boston Globe*, March 7, 2018, https://www.bostonglobe.com/metro/2018/03/07/allegations-employee-mistreatment-roil-renowned-trauma-center/sWW13agQDY9B9A1rt9eqnK/story.html.

13. Bessel van der Kolk, *The Body Keeps the Score: Brain, Mind and Body in the Healing of Trauma* (New York: Penguin Books, 2015), 57.

CHAPTER 7. TOUCH

1. Sheldon Cohen et al., "Does Hugging Provide Stress-Buffering Social Support? A Study of Susceptibility to Upper Respiratory Infection and Illness," *Psychological Science* 26, no. 2 (December 19, 2014): 135–47, https://doi.org/10.1177/0956797614559284.

2. David J. Linden, *Touch: The Science of Hand, Heart, and Mind* (New York: Viking, 2015), 5.

3. Lama Rod Owens, *Love and Rage: The Path of Liberation through Anger* (Berkeley, CA: North Atlantic Books, 2020), 152.

CHAPTER 8. HARM REDUCTION

1. American Psychiatric Association, "What Is PTSD?" August 2020, https://www.psychiatry.org/patients-families/ptsd/what-is-ptsd.

2. Tanya M. Grant, "PTSD and Domestic Violence," *The Encyclopedia of Women and Crime*, August 23, 2019, 1–6, https://doi.org/10.1002/9781118929803.ewac0426.

3. U.S. Department of Veterans Affairs, "Self-Harm and Trauma— PTSD: National Center for PTSD," 2021, https://www.ptsd.va.gov/understand/related/self_harm.asp.

4. Marni Feuerman, "How Stonewalling Harms a Relationship," Verywell Mind, April 9, 2021, https://www.verywellmind.com/coping-when-your-spouse-shuts-down-4097175#citation-3.

5. NDVH Staff, "Is Change Possible in an Abuser?," The Hotline, 2021, https://www.thehotline.org/resources/is-change-possible-in-an-abuser/.

CHAPTER 9. TOOLS FOR HEALING

1. Carmen Maria Machado, *In the Dream House: A Memoir* (Minneapolis: Graywolf Press, 2019), 15.

2. Susan Scrupski, "WHYISTAYED Hashtag Analysis," Big Mountain Data, October 27, 2017, https://www.slideshare.net/BMDVAW/whyistayed-hashtag-analysis.

3. Ralph Garlin Clingan, *Against Cheap Grace in a World Come of Age: An Intellectual Biography of Clayton Powell, 1865–1953* (New York: P. Lang, 2002).

4. Peter A. Levine, *Trauma and Memory: Brain and Body in a Search for the Living Past: A Practical Guide for Understanding and Working with Traumatic Memory* (Berkeley, CA: North Atlantic Books, 2015), 9.

5. David Bullard, "Bessel van Der Kolk on Trauma Interview," Psychotherapy.net, 2014, https://www.psychotherapy.net/interview/bessel-van-der-kolk-trauma.

6. Penny Kaganoff and Susan Spano, eds., *Women on Divorce: A Bedside Companion*, 1st ed (New York: Harcourt Brace, 1995), 9.

CHAPTER 10. GOOD LOVE

1. Erich Fromm, *The Art of Loving* (London: George Allen & Unwin, 1957), 4–5.
2. Stacia L. Brown, "Happiness Happens," *Stacia L. Brown* (blog), August 31, 2015, https://stacialbrown.com/2015/08/31/happiness-happens/

3. Gary D. Chapman and Amy Summers, *The Five Love Languages: How to Express Heartfelt Commitment to Your Mate* (Nashville, TN: Lifeway Press, 2010).

CHAPTER 11. UNSTUCK

1. Lundy Bancroft, *Why Does He Do That? Inside the Minds of Angry and Controlling Men* (New York: Berkley Books, 2003), 12–13.
2. James Gilligan, *Preventing Violence* (London: Thames & Hudson, 2001), 25.
3. Robynne Boyd, "The Heart Yearns for Love," *Goodgrief* (blog), June 21, 2018, https://blog.goodgriefapp.com/2018/06/21/the-heart-yearns-for-love/.
4. Frida Kahlo et al., *The Diary of Frida Kahlo: An Intimate Self-Portrait* (New York: H. N. Abrams, 2005).
5. Toni Cade Bambara, *The Black Woman: An Anthology* (New York: Washington Square Press, 1970), 109–10.

BIBLIOGRAPHY

Adams, Adrienne. "Measuring the Effects of Domestic Violence on Women's Financial Well-Being." Center for Financial Security (CFS Research Brief), 2011. https://centerforfinancialsecurity.files.wordpress.com/2015/04/adams2011.pdf.

American Psychiatric Association. "What Is PTSD?" American Psychiatric Association, August 2020. https://www.psychiatry.org/patients-families/ptsd/what-is-ptsd.

Bambara, Toni Cade. *The Black Woman: An Anthology*. New York: Washington Square Press, 1970.

Bancroft, Lundy. *Why Does He Do That? Inside the Minds of Angry and Controlling Men*. New York: Berkley Books, 2003.

Bever, Lindsey. "'Modern Family' Star Sarah Hyland Gets Restraining Order against Ex-Boyfriend." *Washington Post*, September 25, 2014. https://www.washingtonpost.com/news/morning-mix/wp/2014/09/25/modern-family-star-sarah-hyland-gets-restraining-order-against-ex-boyfriend/.

Bornstein, Robert F. "The Complex Relationship between Dependency and Domestic Violence: Converging Psychological Factors and Social Forces." *American Psychologist* 61, no. 6 (September 2006): 595–606. https://doi.org/10.1037/0003-066x.61.6.595.

Boudouris, J., M. A. Straus, R. J. Gelles, and S. K. Steinmetz. "Behind Closed Doors: Violence in the American Family and Family Violence." *Contemporary Sociology* 11, no. 4 (July 1982). https://doi.org/10.1093/sw/26.4.353.

Boyd, Robynne. "The Heart Yearns for Love." *Goodgrief* (blog), June 21, 2018. https://blog.goodgriefapp.com/2018/06/21/the-heart-yearns-for-love/.

brown, adrienne maree. *Emergent Strategy: Shaping Change, Changing Worlds*. Chico, CA: AK Press, 2017.

Brown, Stacia L. "Happiness Happens." *Stacia L. Brown* (blog), August 31, 2015. https://stacialbrown.com/2015/08/31/happiness-happens/.

Bullard, David. "Bessel van Der Kolk on Trauma Interview." Psychotherapy.net, 2014. https://www.psychotherapy.net/interview/bessel-van-der-kolk-trauma.

Chapman, Gary D., and Amy Summers. *The Five Love Languages: How to Express Heartfelt Commitment to Your Mate*. Nashville, TN: Lifeway Press, 2010.

Chuck, Elizabeth. "The U.S. Finally Has Better Maternal Mortality Data. Can It Now Help Save More Mothers?" *NBC News*, January 29, 2020. https://www.nbcnews.com/health/womens-health/u-s-finally-has-better-maternal-mortality-data-black-mothers-n1125896.

Coates, Ta-Nehisi. "This Town Needs a Better Class of Racist." *The Atlantic*, May 1, 2014. https://www.theatlantic.com/politics/archive/2014/05/This-Town-Needs-A-Better-Class-Of-Racist/361443/.

Cohen, Sheldon, Denise Janicki-Deverts, Ronald B. Turner, and William J. Doyle. "Does Hugging Provide Stress-Buffering Social Support? A Study of Susceptibility to Upper Respiratory Infection and Illness." *Psychological Science* 26, no. 2 (December 19, 2014): 135–47. https://doi.org/10.1177/0956797614559284.

Elsbernd, Mary, and R. Bieringer. *When Love Is Not Enough: A Theo-Ethic of Justice*. Manila, Philippines: Ateneo De Manila University Press, 2008.

Feuerman, Marni. "How Stonewalling Harms a Relationship." Verywell Mind, April 9, 2021. https://www.verywellmind.com/coping-when-your-spouse-shuts-down-4097175#citation-3.

Fromm, Erich. *The Art of Loving*. London: George Allen & Unwin, 1957.

Garlin Clingan, Ralph. *Against Cheap Grace in a World Come of Age: An Intellectual Biography of Clayton Powell, 1865–1953*. New York: P. Lang, 2002.

Gilligan, James. *Preventing Violence*. London: Thames & Hudson, 2001.

Goldstein, Jacob. "How Sunk Cost Fallacy Applies to Love." *National Public Radio*, February 13, 2015. https://choice.npr.org/index.html?origin=https://www.npr.org/2015/02/13/385948508/how-sunk-cost-fallacy-applies-to-love.

Gooden, Beverly. "Why I Created the Why I Stayed (#WhyIStayed) Movement." *Beverly Gooden* (blog), September 8, 2014. https://www.beverlygooden.com/hear/whyistayed.

Grant, Tanya. "Domestic Violence Victims: An Examination of Advocates' Experiences and Impact on Services." *Journal of International Criminal Justice and Legal Issues* 1, no. 1 (2014): 31. https://digitalcommons.sacredheart.edu/cgi/viewcontent.cgi?article=1019&context=cj_fac.

Grant, Tanya M. "PTSD and Domestic Violence." *The Encyclopedia of Women and Crime*, August 23, 2019, 1–6. https://doi.org/10.1002/9781118929803.ewac0426.

Hassanein, Nada. "Florida Protester Oluwatoyin Salau Killed in Tallahassee after Going Missing." *Tallahassee Democrat*, June 15, 2020. https://www.tallahassee.com/story/news/2020/06/15/oluwatoyin-salau-found-dead-tallahassee-black-lives-matter-protest-missing/3190021001/.

Institute Staff. "11 Terms You Should Know to Better Understand Structural Racism." The Aspen Institute, August 29, 2017. https://www.aspeninstitute.org/blog-posts/structural-racism-definition/.

Johnson, Morgan Brewton. "Once Again, Black Women Are Heroes. It's Time to Pay Up." *WBUR*, February 8, 2021. https://www.wbur.org/cognoscenti/2021/02/08/black-women-stacey-abrams-kamala-harris-morgan-brewton-johnson.

Kaganoff, Penny, and Susan Spano, eds. *Women on Divorce: A Bedside Companion*. 1st ed. New York: Harcourt Brace, 1995.

Kahlo, Frida, Carlos Fuentes, Sarah M. Lowe, and Phyllis Freeman. *The Diary of Frida Kahlo: An Intimate Self-Portrait*. New York: H. N. Abrams, 2005.

Kamin, Debra. "Black Homeowners Face Discrimination in Appraisals." *New York Times*, August 27, 2020, https://www.nytimes.com/2020/08/25/realestate/blacks-minorities-appraisals-discrimination.html.

Kendall, Mikki. *Hood Feminism: Notes from the Women That a Movement Forgot*. New York: Penguin Books, 2021.

Kowalczyk, Liz. "Allegations of Employee Mistreatment Roil Renowned Brookline Trauma Center." *Boston Globe*, March 7, 2018. https://www.bostonglobe.com/me-

tro/2018/03/07/allegations-employee-mistreatment-roil-renowned-trauma-center/
sWW13agQDY9B9A1rt9eqnK/story.html.

Lee, Trymaine. "How America's Vast Racial Wealth Gap Grew: By Plunder." *New York Times*, August 14, 2019. https://www.nytimes.com/interactive/2019/08/14/magazine/racial-wealth-gap.html.

Levine, Peter A. *Trauma and Memory: Brain and Body in a Search for the Living Past: A Practical Guide for Understanding and Working with Traumatic Memory*. Berkeley, CA: North Atlantic Books, 2015.

Linden, David J. *Touch: The Science of Hand, Heart, and Mind*. New York: Viking, 2015.

Lindsey, Treva. "The Urgent Crisis of Missing Black Women and Girls." Women's Media Center, February 20, 2020. https://womensmediacenter.com/news-features/the-urgent-crisis-of-missing-black-women-and-girls.

Logan, Erin. "A Florida Bank Refused to Cash an Elderly Black Woman's Check. Then They Called the Police on Her." *The Independent*, July 28, 2018. https://www.independent.co.uk/news/fargo-wells-bank-black-woman-cheque-florida-barbara-carroll-discrimination-a8467596.html.

Machado, Carmen Maria. *In the Dream House: A Memoir*. Minneapolis: Graywolf Press, 2019.

Malkin, Craig. "Why Do People Stay in Abusive Relationships?" *Psychology Today*, 2013. https://www.psychologytoday.com/us/blog/romance-redux/201303/why-do-people-stay-in-abusive-relationships.

Miles-Doan, Rebecca. "Violence between Spouses and Intimates: Does Neighborhood Context Matter?" *Social Forces* 77, no. 2 (December 1998): 623. https://doi.org/10.2307/3005541.

NDVH Staff. "Is Change Possible in an Abuser?" The Hotline, 2021. https://www.thehotline.org/resources/is-change-possible-in-an-abuser/.

Owens, Lama Rod. *Love and Rage: The Path of Liberation through Anger*. Berkeley, CA: North Atlantic Books, 2020.

Richie, Beth E. "A Black Feminist Reflection on the Antiviolence Movement." *Signs: Journal of Women in Culture and Society* 25, no. 4 (July 2000): 1133–37. https://doi.org/10.1086/495533.

Roeder, Amy. "America Is Failing Its Black Mothers." *Harvard Public Health Magazine*, December 21, 2018. https://www.hsph.harvard.edu/magazine/magazine_article/america-is-failing-its-black-mothers/.

Sampson, Robert J., and William Julius Wilson. "Toward a Theory of Race, Crime, and Urban Inequality." In *Crime and Inequality*, edited by John Hagan and Ruth D. Peterson, 44. Stanford, CA: Stanford University Press, 1995.

Scrupski, Susan. "WHYISTAYED Hashtag Analysis." Big Mountain Data, October 27, 2017. https://www.slideshare.net/BMDVAW/whyistayed-hashtag-analysis.

Smith, Michael D. "Sociodemographic Risk Factors in Wife Abuse: Results from a Survey of Toronto Women." *Canadian Journal of Sociology / Cahiers Canadiens de Sociologie* 15, no. 1 (1990): 39. https://doi.org/10.2307/3341172.

Sokoloff, Natalie J., and Ida Dupont. "Domestic Violence at the Intersections of Race, Class, and Gender." *Violence against Women* 11, no. 1 (January 2005): 38–64. https://doi.org/10.1177/1077801204271476.

Steiner, Leslie Morgan. "Why Domestic Violence Victims Don't Leave." TED Talks, 2013. https://www.ted.com/talks/leslie_morgan_steiner_why_domestic_violence_victims_don_t_leave.

Stieb, Matt. "What We Know about the Death of Black Lives Matter Activist Oluwatoyin Salau." *Intelligencer*, June 16, 2020. https://nymag.com/intelligencer/2020/06/what-we-know-about-the-death-of-activist-oluwatoyin-salau.html.

Tulsa Historical Society and Museum. "1921 Tulsa Race Massacre." Tulsa Historical Society and Museum, November 2018. https://www.tulsahistory.org/exhibit/1921-tulsa-race-massacre/.

Urban Institute. "Structural Racism in America." Urban Institute, September 21, 2016. https://www.urban.org/features/structural-racism-america.

U.S. Department of Veterans Affairs. "Self-Harm and Trauma—PTSD: National Center for PTSD." U.S. Department of Veterans Affairs, 2021. https://www.ptsd.va.gov/understand/related/self_harm.asp.

van der Kolk, Bessel. *The Body Keeps the Score: Brain, Mind and Body in the Healing of Trauma*. New York: Penguin Books, 2015.

INDEX

abuse: definition, 7; patterns, 7
abusers, 186–187
abusive behaviors, 145; apology in, 147; awareness of, 145–146; change in, 146–147; defense mechanisms in, 147; facing ourselves in, 146
acceptance of where you are: about holding space, 129–130; about pain, 129; about touch, 128–129
accidents, 6
accountability, 66; in reinvention, 112–113; in thoughts on forgiveness, 161
accusations, 1; from husband, 7–8, 17; from marriage counselor, 24–25
adaptation, 19
admitting, to violent abuse, 38
adoption, 106
African proverb, 133
agency, 2
Alex, 25
All About Love (hooks), 173
Allstate Foundation's Purple Purse initiative, 71
Anderson, Jamie, 188
anger, 130–131
appearance, 115
appeasement, 18–19

arguments, 36, 42–43
aromatherapy, 142
The Art of Loving (Fromm), 168–169
Association for Psychological Science, 122
attention, 126. *See also* reactions, paying attention to
attentiveness, 12, 13
attorneys, 75, 80
awakening, 39

Bailey, Moya, 73
Bambara, Toni Cade, 189–190
Bancroft, Lundy, 186
beauty, 13, 159; of living, 195; from pain, 189; of rebuilding, 185; of resolution, 191
being, 116
The Belief in a Just World (Lerner), 67
birth control, 114, 143, 144
The Black Woman (Bambara), 189–190
Black women, 178; in academia, 56; being seen, 62; deaths of, 74–75; disappearance of, 63, 74, 96–97; Nigerian school girls as, 96–97; structural racism and, 72, 73; in theory of justice, 89
blame, 70